THE
MEMORY
JOGGER™ II
Healthcare
Edition

A Pocket Guide of
Tools for Continuous
Improvement and
Effective Planning

First Edition

GOAL/QPC

The Memory Jogger™ II Healthcare Edition

Development Team

Michael Brassard, *Author*

Diane Ritter, *Author*

Deborah Crovo, *Graphics*

Michele Kierstead, *Layout Production*

Janet MacCausland, *Cover Design*

Francine Oddo, *Editor*

Dan Picard, *Editor*

GOALQPC

GOAL/QPC | Memory Jogger
8E Industrial Way, Suite 3, Salem, NH 03079
Toll free: 800.643.4316 or 603.893.1944
service@goalqpc.com
MemoryJogger.org

Printed in the United States of America

First Edition
10 9 8 7 6 5 4 3

ISBN 978-1-57681-079-8

Acknowledgments

Our sincerest appreciation and thanks go to our dedicated, knowledgeable, and tireless friends who have worked so hard to make this little book a BIG success.

Production & Administrative Staff: Lee Alphen, Steve Boudreau, Paul Brassard, Lori Champney, Deborah Crovo, Brian Hettrick, Michele Kierstead, Rob King, Fran Kudzia, Larry LeFebre, Janet MacCausland, Francine Oddo, Dorie Overhoff, Dan Picard, & Debra Vartanian.

Concept & Content Reviewers: Del Bassett, Casey Collett, Ann McManus, Bill Montgomery, Bob Porter, Paul Ritter, & Sharon Muret-Wagstaff.

Customers & Collaborators: To the customer focus groups for their insights and suggestions.

Companies Who Contributed Information for Illustrations:
The American Association of Colleges of Pharmacy; Tony Borgen & Paul Hearn, *Hamilton Standard*; Lisa Boisvert, *Business Centered Learning, LLC*; COLA; Nicholas Governale; Kirk Kochenberger, *Parkview Episcopal Medical Center*; Patti Gasdek Manolakis, *PMM Consulting*; Weston F. Milliken, *CUE Consulting*; *Partners HealthCare System*; Jim Salsbury; Marie Sinioris, *Rush-Presbyterian-St. Luke's Medical Center*; Jann B. Skelton, *Silver Pennies Consulting*; Capt. T. C. Splitgerber, *U.S. Navy, Naval Dental Center, San Diego*; Staff Team Members, *Park Nicollet Clinic HealthSystems Minnesota*; Staff Team Members, *Trinity Health Systems, Inc.*; Natalie Twaddel, RN, BSN, RNC; Jack Waddell, *Novacor Chemicals*; Kemper Watkins, MSgt., *U.S. Air Force, Air Combat Command*.

How to Use This Book

The Memory Jogger™ II: Healthcare Edition is designed for you to use as a convenient and quick reference guide on the job. Put your finger on any tool within seconds!

Know the tool you need? Find it by using the:

Table of Contents. The tools and techniques are in alphabetical order.

Solid tab. Look for the blue box at the bottom of the first page of each new section.

Not sure what tool you need? Get an idea by using the:

Tool Selector Chart. This chart organizes the tools by typical improvement situations, such as working with numbers, with ideas, or in teams.

What do the different positions of runners mean?

🏃• **Getting Ready**—An important first step is to select the right tool for the situation. When you see the "getting ready" position of the runner, expect a brief description of the tool's purpose and a list of benefits in using the tool.

🏃 **Cruising**—When you see this runner, expect to find construction guidelines and interpretation tips. This is the action phase that provides you with step-by-step instructions and helpful formulas.

🏃 **Finishing the Course**—When you see this runner, expect to see the tool in its final form. View examples to see how each tool can be applied specifically to health care.

Foreword

Clinicians, leaders, and all of us who work from the front line to the back office have an unprecedented opportunity to make health care all that we dreamed it could be when we first entered the field. With our burgeoning evidence base, access to information and new technology, and superb cadre of colleagues from diverse disciplines, we can answer the call of the Institute of Medicine to make all of health care:

- Safe,

- Effective,

- Patient-centered,

- Timely,

- Efficient, and

- Equitable

for every person, every time.

At the same time, our challenge increases with the growing size and complexity of our organizations and health systems. We put our mission first, but too often find that the implementation of good ideas lags behind.

Fortunately, people in other fields have faced similar challenges and we can borrow and adapt their tools and approaches to bring about dramatic improvements. In this handy pocket guide, you will find a wealth of easy-to-use examples and tips to do just that. In fact, an increasing number of healthcare contributors are now "giving back" to the manufacturing and service industries that developed and tested these ideas originally. Whether your current focus is on a simple process or a key result, whether you are working individually or leading a team or an entire institution, you will find examples that will help you move better, faster, and with greater ease and joy toward your goals. Frequently, you will find ways to reduce costs as well. The more resources you save, the more you can drive into the mission.

As you go forward in making health care all that it can be for the patients and families you serve, here are several suggestions from people in healthcare organizations just like yours:

1. Keep patients first.

2. Keep it simple. Many have succeeded in mastering critical changes with little more than quick, repeated Plan, Do, Check, Act Cycles.

3. Bring everyone affected onto the team—including the patients. Capturing knowledge from multiple perspectives will help you create stronger systems and results.

4. Focus not only on individual processes but also on leadership, strategy, stakeholders, measurement and knowledge management, staff needs, and short- and long-term results.

5. Consider core values and concepts from the Baldrige National Quality Program in developing your own. These include visionary leadership, patient-focused excellence, organizational and personal learning, valuing of staff and partners, agility, focus on the future, managing for innovation, management by fact, social responsibility and community health, focus on results and creating value, and systems perspective. Be a borrower!

Best wishes to you and your colleagues as you strive to meet your goals. We hope that you will become a contributor in the future to these tools and examples that are helping others create high-performing organizations in health care.

Sharon Muret-Wagstaff, PhD, MPA

Assistant Professor of Pediatrics
Harvard Medical School

Contents

Tool Selector Chart

This chart organizes the tools by typical improvement situations, such as working with numbers, with ideas, or in teams.

Working with Ideas	Page #	Generating/Grouping	Deciding	Implementing
AND	3			●
Affinity	12	●		
Brainstorming	19	●		
C & E/Fishbone	23	●	●	
Flowchart	56	●	●	●
Force Field	63	●	●	
Gantt	9			●
ID	76	●	●	
Matrix	85			●
NGT/Multivoting	91		●	
Prioritization	105		●	
PDPC	143			●
Radar	120		●	
Tree	139	●		●

# #

Working with Numbers	Page #	Counting	Measures
Check Sheet	31		
Control Charts	36		
Data Points	52		
Histogram	66		
Pareto	95		
Process Capability	115		
Run	124		
Scatter	128		

Working in Teams	Page #	Improvement Road Map	Team Road Map
Starting Teams	133		
Maintaining Momentum	134		
Ending Teams/Projects	136		
Effective Meetings	137		
Storyboard Case Study	148		

Introduction

From classrooms to board rooms, on manufacturing floors and in medical centers, organizations around the world are using *continuous quality improvement (CQI)* as their strategy to bring about dramatic changes in their operations. Their purpose is to stay competitive in a world of instant communication and technological advancement.

These organizations need to meet or exceed customer expectations while maintaining a cost-competitive position. *Continuous quality improvement (CQI)*, a systematic, organization-wide approach for continually improving all processes that deliver quality products and services, is the strategy many organizations are adopting to meet today's challenges and to prepare for those down the road.

In pursuing CQI, stick to these four basic principles:

1. Develop a strong customer focus.
2. Continually improve all processes.
3. Involve employees.
4. Mobilize both data *and* team knowledge to improve decision making.

1. **Develop a strong customer focus.**

   Total customer focus includes the needs of both external and internal customers. External customers are the end users, internal customers are your coworkers and other departments in the organization.

2. **Continually improve all processes.**

   • *Identify them.* A process is a sequence of repeatable steps that lead to some desired end or output: a typed document, a printed circuit board, a "home-cooked" meal, arrival at work, and so on.

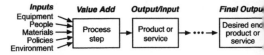

Inputs
Equipment
People
Materials
Policies
Environment

Value Add

Process step

Output/Input

Product or service

Final Output

Desired end product or service

- *Improve them.* Use the **Plan, Do, Check, Act (PDCA) Cycle: PLAN** what you want to accomplish over a period of time and what you might do, or need to do to get there. **DO** what you planned on doing. Start on a small scale! **CHECK** the results of what you did to see if the objective was achieved. **ACT** on the information. If you were successful, standardize the plan; otherwise, continue in the cycle to plan for further improvement.

3. **Involve employees.**

Encourage teams—train them—support them—use their work—celebrate their accomplishments!

4. **Mobilize both data and team knowledge to improve decision making.**

Use the tools to get the most out of your data and the knowledge of your team members.

- Graphically display number and word data; team members can easily uncover patterns within the data, and immediately focus on the most important targets for improvement.
- Develop team consensus on the root cause(s) of a problem and on the plan for improvement.
- Provide a safe and efficient outlet for ideas at all levels.

Use this book and the tools in it to focus on, improve, involve employees in, and direct your path toward continuous quality improvement.

Activity Network Diagram (AND)
Scheduling sequential & simultaneous tasks

Why use it?

To allow a team to find both the most efficient path and realistic schedule for the completion of any project by graphically showing total completion time, the necessary sequence of tasks, those tasks that can be done simultaneously, and the critical tasks to monitor.

What does it do?

- All team members have a chance to give a realistic picture of what their piece of the plan requires, based on real experience
- Everyone sees why he or she is critical to the overall success of the project
- Unrealistic implementation timetables are discovered and adjusted in the planning stage
- The entire team can think creatively about how to shorten tasks that are bottlenecks
- The entire team can focus its attention and scarce resources on the truly critical tasks

How do I do it?

1. **Assemble the right team of people with firsthand knowledge of the subtasks.**

2. **Brainstorm or document all the tasks needed to complete a project. Record on sticky notes.**

---

3. **Find the first task that must be done, and place the card on the extreme left of a large work surface.**

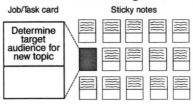

4. **Ask: "Are there any tasks that can be done simultaneously with task #1?"**

   • If there are simultaneous tasks, place the task card above or below task #1. If not, go to the next step.

5. **Ask, "What is the next task that must be done? Can others be done simultaneously?"**

   • Repeat this questioning process until all the recorded tasks are placed in sequence and in parallel.

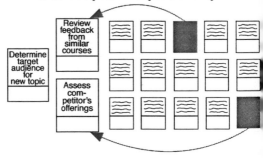

Tip At each step always ask, "Have we forgotten any other needed tasks that could be done simultaneously?"

6. **Number each task, draw the connecting arrows, and agree on a realistic time for the completion of each task.**

   - Record the completion time on the bottom half of each card.

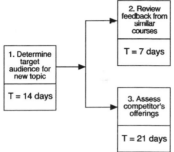

   Tip Be sure to agree on the standard time unit for each task (e.g., days, weeks). Elapsed time is easier than "dedicated" time (e.g., 8 hours of dedicated time versus 8 hours over a two-week period (elapsed time)).

7. **Determine the project's critical path.**

   - Any delay to a task on the *critical path* will be added to the project's completion time, unless another task is accelerated or eliminated. Likewise, the project's completion time can be reduced by accelerating any task on the critical path.

   - There are two options for calculating the total critical path and the tasks included within it.

     Longest cumulative path. Identify total project completion time. Add up each path of connected activities. The longest cumulative path is the quickest possible implementation time. This is the project's *critical path*.

Calculated slack. Calculate the "slack" in the starting and completion times of each task. This identifies which tasks must be completed exactly as scheduled (on the *critical path*) and those that have some latitude.

Finding the critical path by calculating the slack

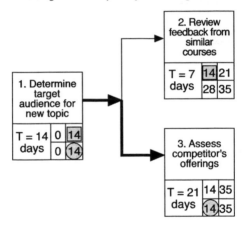

Earliest Start (ES)	Earliest Finish (EF)	ES = The *largest* EF of any *previous* connected task
Latest Start (LS)	Latest Finish (LF)	EF = ES + the time to complete that task

ES = The *largest* EF of any *previous* connected task

EF = ES + the time to complete that task

LS = LF - the time to complete that task

LF = The *smallest* LS of any connected *following* task

When ES = LS AND EF = LF, that task is on the critical path, and therefore there is no schedule flexibility in this task.

Tip Determining the longest cumulative path is simpler than calculating the slack, but can quickly become confusing in larger ANDs.

The calculated slack option determines the total project and slack times; and therefore the total project time and critical path are identified "automatically."

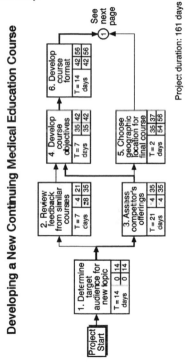

Developing a New Continuing Medical Education Course

Project duration: 161 days

See next page

Developing a New Continuing Medical Education Course (continued)

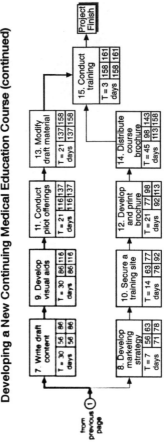

©1994, 2005, 2008 GOAL/QPC

Variations

The constructed example shown in this section is in the Activity on Node (AON) format. For more information on other formats such as Activity on Arrow (AOA) and Precedence Diagram (PDM), see *The Memory Jogger Plus+®*.

Another widely used, schedule-monitoring method is the Gantt Chart. It is a simple tool that uses horizontal bars to show which tasks can be done simultaneously over the life of the project.

Developing a New Continuing Medical Education Course

ID	Name	Jan.	Feb.	Mar.	April	May	June
A	Determine target audience for new topic						
B	Assess competitor's offerings						
C	Develop course objectives						
D	Develop course format						
E	Write draft content						
F	Develop visual aids						
G	Conduct pilot offerings						
H	Modify draft materials						
I	Conduct training						

Project duration: 161 days

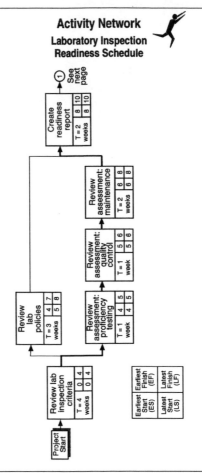

Activity Network

**Laboratory Inspection
Readiness Schedule**

See next page

Create readiness report

T = 2 weeks | 8 | 10
 | 8 | 10

Review assessment: maintenance

T = 2 weeks | 6 | 8
 | 6 | 8

Review assessment: quality control

T = 1 week | 5 | 6
 | 5 | 6

Review lab policies

T = 3 weeks | 4 | 7
 | 5 | 8

Review assessment: proficiency testing

T = 1 week | 4 | 5
 | 4 | 5

Review lab inspection criteria

T = 4 weeks | 0 | 4
 | 0 | 4

Project Start

Earliest Start (ES) | Earliest Finish (EF)
Latest Start (LS) | Latest Finish (LF)

©1994, 2005, 2008 GOAL/QPC

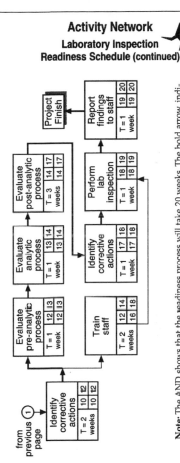

Identify corrective actions (from previous page ①) — T = 2 weeks | 10 | 12 | 10 | 12

Evaluate pre-analytic process — T = 1 week | 12 | 13 | 12 | 13

Evaluate analytic process — T = 1 week | 13 | 14 | 13 | 14

Evaluate post-analytic process — T = 3 weeks | 14 | 17 | 14 | 17

Train staff — T = 2 weeks | 12 | 14 | 16 | 18

Identify corrective actions — T = 1 week | 17 | 18 | 17 | 18

Perform lab inspection — T = 1 week | 18 | 19 | 18 | 19

Report findings to staff — T = 1 week | 19 | 20 | 19 | 20

Project Finish

Note: The AND shows that the readiness process will take 20 weeks. The bold arrow, indicating the critical path, clearly shows those tasks that must be completed as scheduled. The tasks off the critical path will also require careful monitoring because there are only five weeks of slack time in the schedule.

 **Affinity Diagram**
Gathering & grouping ideas

Why use it?

To allow a team to creatively generate a large number of ideas/issues and then organize and summarize natural groupings among them to understand the essence of a problem and breakthrough solutions.

What does it do?

- Encourages creativity by everyone on the team at all phases of the process
- Breaks down long-standing communication barriers
- Encourages nontraditional connections among ideas/issues
- Allows breakthroughs to emerge naturally, even on long-standing issues
- Encourages "ownership" of results that emerge because the team creates both the detailed input and general results
- Overcomes "team paralysis," which is brought on by an overwhelming array of options and lack of consensus

How do I do it?

1. **Phrase the issue under discussion in a full sentence.**

> What issues are involved in creating/enforcing
> a standard ventilator-care process?

©1994, 2005, 2008 GOAL/QPC

Tip From the start, reach consensus on the choice of words you will use. Neutral statements work well, but positive, negative, and solution-oriented questions also work.

2. Brainstorm at least 20 ideas or issues.

a) Follow guidelines for brainstorming.

b) Record each idea on a sticky note in bold, large print to make it visible 4–6 feet away. Use, at minimum, a noun and a verb. Avoid using single words. Four to seven words work well.

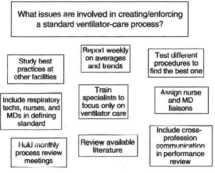

| What issues are involved in creating/enforcing a standard ventilator-care process? |

Study best practices at other facilities	Report weekly on averages and trends	Test different procedures to find the best one
Include respiratory techs, nurses, and MDs in defining standard	Train specialists to focus only on ventilator care	Assign nurse and MD liaisons
Hold monthly process review meetings	Review available literature	Include cross-profession communication in performance review

Illustration Note: There are 10 to 40 more ideas in a typical Affinity Diagram.

Tip A "typical" Affinity has 40–60 items; it is not unusual to have 100–200 ideas.

3. Without talking: sort ideas simultaneously into 5–10 related groupings.

a) Move sticky notes where they fit best for you; don't ask, simply move any notes that you think belong in another grouping.

b) Sorting will slow down or stop when each person feels sufficiently comfortable with the groupings.

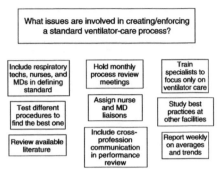

> What issues are involved in creating/enforcing a standard ventilator-care process?

Include respiratory techs, nurses, and MDs in defining standard	Hold monthly process review meetings	Train specialists to focus only on ventilator care
Test different procedures to find the best one	Assign nurse and MD liaisons	Study best practices at other facilities
Review available literature	Include cross-profession communication in performance review	Report weekly on averages and trends

Illustration Note: There are 5 to 10 more groupings of ideas in a typical Affinity Diagram.

Tip Sort in silence to focus on the meaning behind and connections among all ideas, instead of emotions and "history" that often arise in discussions.

Tip As an idea is moved back and forth, try to see the logical connection that the other person is making. If this movement continues beyond a reasonable point, agree to create a duplicate sticky note.

Tip It is okay for some notes to stand alone. These "loners" can be as important as others that fit into groupings naturally.

4. **For each grouping, create summary or header cards using consensus.**

a) Gain a quick team consensus on a word or phrase that captures the central idea/theme of each grouping; record it on a sticky note and place it at the top of each grouping. These are *draft* header cards.

b) For each grouping, agree on a concise sentence that combines the grouping's central idea and what all of the specific sticky notes add to that idea; record it and replace the draft version. This is a final header card.

c) Divide large groupings into subgroups as needed and create appropriate subheaders.

d) Draw the final Affinity Diagram connecting all finalized header cards with their groupings.

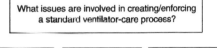

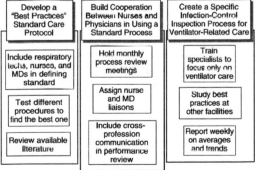

Information provided courtesy of Lisa Boisvert, Business Centered Learning, LLC

Illustration Note: There are 5 to 10 groupings of ideas in a typical Affinity. This is a partial Affinity.

Tip Spend the extra time needed to do solid header cards. Strive to capture the essence of *all* of the ideas in each grouping. ***Shortcuts here can greatly reduce the effectiveness of the final Affinity Diagram.***

It is possible that a note within a grouping could become a header card. However, don't choose the "closest one" because it's convenient. The hard work of creating new header cards often leads to breakthrough ideas.

Variations

Another popular form of this tool, called the KJ Method, was developed by the Japanese anthropologist Jiro Kawakita while he was doing fieldwork in the 1950s. The KJ Method, identified with Kawakita's initials, helped the anthropologist and his students gather and analyze data. The KJ Method differs from the Affinity Diagram described above in that the cards are fact-based and go through a highly structured refinement process before the final diagram is created.

Affinity

Challenges to Improving Clinical Education

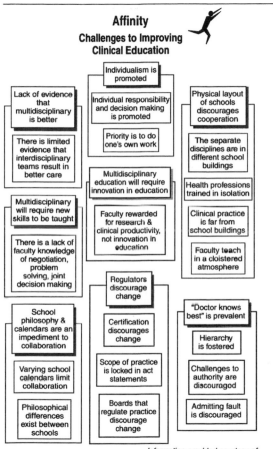

Individualism is promoted

Individual responsibility and decision making is promoted

Priority is to do one's own work

Lack of evidence that multidisciplinary is better

There is limited evidence that interdisciplinary teams result in better care

Multidisciplinary will require new skills to be taught

There is a lack of faculty knowledge of negotiation, problem solving, joint decision making

Multidisciplinary education will require innovation in education

Faculty rewarded for research & clinical productivity, not innovation in education

Physical layout of schools discourages cooperation

The separate disciplines are in different school buildings

Health professions trained in isolation

Clinical practice is far from school buildings

Faculty teach in a cloistered atmosphere

School philosophy & calendars are an impediment to collaboration

Varying school calendars limit collaboration

Philosophical differences exist between schools

Regulators discourage change

Certification discourages change

Scope of practice is locked in act statements

Boards that regulate practice discourage change

"Doctor knows best" is prevalent

Hierarchy is fostered

Challenges to authority are discouraged

Admitting fault is discouraged

Information provided courtesy of
The American Association of Colleges of Pharmacy (AACP)

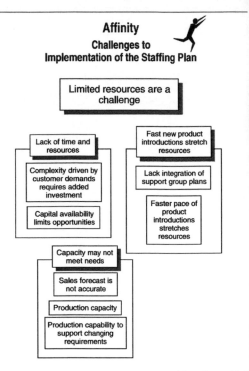

Affinity

Challenges to
Implementation of the Staffing Plan

Limited resources are a challenge

Lack of time and resources

Complexity driven by customer demands requires added investment

Capital availability limits opportunities

Fast new product introductions stretch resources

Lack integration of support group plans

Faster pace of product introductions stretches resources

Capacity may not meet needs

Sales forecast is not accurate

Production capacity

Production capability to support changing requirements

*Information provided
courtesy of Natalie Twaddel, RN, BSN, RNC*

 **Brainstorming**
*Creating bigger
& better ideas*

Why use it?

To establish a common method for a team to creatively
and efficiently generate a high volume of ideas on any
topic by creating a process that is free of criticism and
judgment.

What does it do?

- Encourages open thinking when a team is stuck in
  "same old way" thinking
- Gets all team members involved and enthusiastic
  so that a few people don't dominate the whole
  group
- Allows team members to build on each other's
  creativity while staying focused on their joint
  mission

How do I do it?

There are two major methods for brainstorming.

- *Structured.* A process in which each team member
  gives ideas in turn.
- *Unstructured.* A process in which team members
  give ideas as they come to mind.

Either method can be done silently or aloud.

Structured

1. **The central brainstorming question is stated, agreed on, and written down for everyone to see.**

   Be sure that everyone understands the question, issue, or problem. Check this by asking one or two members to paraphrase it before recording it on a flipchart or board.

2. **Each team member, in turn, gives an idea. No idea is criticized. Ever!**

   With each rotation around the team, any member can pass at any time. While this rotation process encourages full participation, it may also heighten anxiety for inexperienced or shy team members.

3. **As ideas are generated, write each one in large, visible letters on a flipchart or other writing surface.**

   Make sure every idea is recorded with the same words of the speaker; don't interpret or abbreviate. To ensure this, the person writing should always ask the speaker if the idea has been worded accurately.

4. **Ideas are generated in turn until each person passes, indicating that the ideas (or members) are exhausted.**

   Keep the process moving and relatively short— 5 to 20 minutes works well, depending on how complex the topic is.

5. **Review the written list of ideas for clarity and discard any duplicates.**

   Discard only ideas that are virtually identical. It is often important to preserve subtle differences that are revealed in slightly different wordings.

Unstructured

The process is the same as in the structured method except that ideas are given by everyone at any time. There is no need to "pass" because ideas are not solicited in rotation.

Variations

There are many ways to stimulate creative team thinking. The common theme among all of them is the stimulation of creativity by taking advantage of the combined brainpower of a team. Here are three examples:

- **Visual brainstorming.** Individuals (or the team) produce a picture of how they see a situation or problem.

- **Analogies/free-word association.** Unusual connections are made by comparing the problem to seemingly unrelated objects, creatures, or words. For example: "If the problem was an animal, what kind would it be?"

- **6-3-5 method.** This powerful, silent method is proposed by Helmut Schlicksupp in his book *Creativity Workshop*. It is done as follows:

  a) Based on a single brainstorming issue, each person on the team (usually 6 people) has 5 minutes to write down 3 ideas on a sheet of paper.

  b) Each person then passes his or her sheet of paper to the next person, who has 5 more minutes to add 3 more ideas that build on the first 3 ideas.

  c) This rotation is repeated as many times as there are team members (e.g., 6 team members = 6 rotations, 6 sheets of paper, 18 ideas per sheet).

  This interesting process forces team members to consciously build on each other's perspectives and input.

Example of a Brainstorming Session with the Facilitator's Commentary

Practice in brainstorming will help team members learn how best to make contributions. The following example shows a sample of ideas and the facilitator's evaluation of each idea's quality and appropriateness to the problem. There are four participants (Jim, Bob, Lisa, and Lynn) and one facilitator in this brainstorming session. The example shows the participants' ideas on the left and the facilitator's comments in the balloons. The example follows the session up to the first period of silence or "dead point."

Facilitator's Commentary on Ideas for Childproofing Medicine Containers

Jim: What if you have to push down and turn the cover at the same time to open?

Lisa: Or push in side tab(s) and turn the cover at the same time to open.

Jim: What about having arrows line up and push up?

Lynn: Or a combination lock. You might need to turn the cover to a certain number to open

Lisa: What if you needed to push in a release button on the bottom of the bottle while turning the cover to open?

> Any idea is a good idea!

Or what if the cover sticks to your fingers if opened incorrectly?

> These comments show the flow of ideas, leapfrogging off each other.

Bob: How about simply making use of adults' greater strength, and making the top hard to turn?

Lynn: That wouldn't work. People who aren't strong enough couldn't manage!

> Voicing of criticism

Let me restate that last comment. One advantage would be the simplicity of that idea. But how would, say, people with less strength be able to manage?

> Looks at the positives and then addresses concerns.

Jim: A special key could be included with the package that would allow them to increase the force they can apply.

> Constructive response to the concern

**Cause & Effect/
Fishbone Diagram**
*Find & cure causes,
NOT symptoms*

Why use it?

To allow a team to identify, explore, and graphically display, in increasing detail, all of the possible causes related to a problem or condition to discover its root cause(s).

What does it do?

- Enables a team to focus on the content of the problem, not on the history of the problem or differing personal interests of team members
- Creates a snapshot of the collective knowledge and consensus of a team around a problem. This builds support for the resulting solutions
- Focuses the team on causes, not symptoms

How do I do it?

1. **Select the most appropriate cause & effect format. There are two major formats:**

   - The **Dispersion Analysis Type** is constructed by placing individual causes within each "major" cause category and then asking of each individual cause "Why does this cause (dispersion) happen?" This question is repeated for the next level of detail until the team runs out of causes. The graphic examples shown in Step 3 of this tool section are based on this format.

- The **Process Classification Type** uses the major steps of the process in place of the major cause categories. The root cause questioning process is the same as the Dispersion Analysis Type.

2. **Generate the causes needed to build a Cause & Effect Diagram. Choose one method:**
   - **Brainstorming** without previous preparation
   - **Check Sheets** based on data collected by team members before the meeting

3. **Construct the Cause & Effect/Fishbone Diagram.**
   a) Place the problem statement in a box on the righthand side of the writing surface.
   - Allow plenty of space. Use a flipchart sheet, butcher paper, or a large white board. A paper surface is preferred to allow the final Cause & Effect Diagram to be moved.

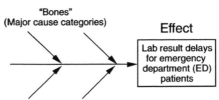

Causes

"Bones"
(Major cause categories)

Effect

Lab result delays for emergency department (ED) patients

Tip Make sure everyone agrees on the problem statement. Include as much information as possible on the "what," "where," "when," and "how much" of the problem. Use data to specify the problem.

b) Draw major cause categories or steps in the production or service process. Connect them to the "backbone" of the fishbone chart.

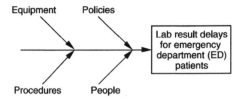

Illustration Note: In a Process Classification Type format, replace the major "bone" categories with: "Preparation," "Specimen Collection," "Analysis," and "Reporting."

- Be flexible in the major cause "bones" that are used. In a **Production Process** the traditional categories are: **Machines** (equipment), **Methods** (how work is done), **Materials** (components or raw materials), and **People** (the human element). In a **Service Process** the traditional methods are: **Policies** (higher-level decision rules), **Procedures** (steps in a task), **Plant** (equipment and space), and **People**. In both types of processes, **Environment** (buildings, logistics, and space), and **Measurement** (calibration and data collection) are also frequently used. *There is no perfect set or number of categories. Make them fit the problem.*

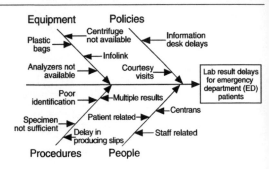

Equipment   Policies

Plastic bags

Centrifuge not available

Information desk delays

Infolink

Analyzers not available

Courtesy visits

Lab result delays for emergency department (ED) patients

Poor identification

Multiple results

Centrans

Specimen not sufficient

Patient related

Delay in producing slips

Staff related

Procedures   People

c) Place the brainstormed or data-based causes in the appropriate category.

- In brainstorming, possible causes can be placed in a major cause category as each is generated, or only after the entire list has been created. Either works well but brainstorming the whole list first maintains the creative flow of ideas without being constrained by the major cause categories or where the ideas fit in each "bone."

- Some causes seem to fit in more than one category. Ideally each cause should be in only one category, but some of the "people" causes may legitimately belong in two places. Place them in both categories and see how they work out in the end.

Tip If ideas are slow in coming, use the major cause categories as catalysts (e.g., "What in 'policies' is causing . . . ?")

d) Ask repeatedly of each cause listed on the "bones," either

- "Why does it happen?" For example, under "Centrifuge not available," this question would lead to more basic causes such as "Broken," "In process," and so on.

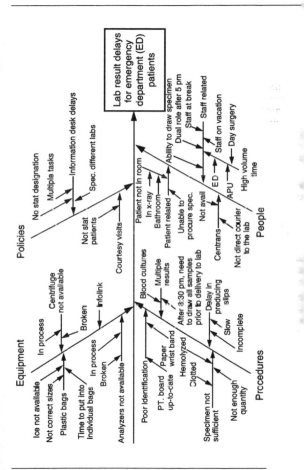

Lab result delays for emergency department (ED) patients

Policies
- No stat designation
- Multiple tasks
- Information desk delays
- Spec. different labs
- Not stat patients
- Courtesy visits

People
- Patient not in room
  - In x-ray
  - Bathroom
  - Patient related
- Ability to draw specimen
- Dual role after 5 pm
- Staff at break
- Staff related
- Staff on vacation
- Day surgery
- Unable to procure spec.
- Not avail
  - ED
  - APU
- High volume time
- Not direct courier to the lab
- Centrans

Equipment
- Ice not available
- Not correct sizes
- Plastic bags
  - Time to put into
  - Individual bags
- In process
- Centrifuge not available
- Broken
- In process
- Broken
- Infolink
- Analyzers not available

Procedures
- Poor Identification
  - PT. board up-to-date
  - Paper wrist band
- Blood cultures
- Multiple results
- After 3:30 pm, need to draw all samples prior to delivery to lab
- Delay in producing slips
- Slow
- Incomplete
- Hemolyzed
- Clotted
- Specimen not sufficient
- Not enough quantity

- "What could happen?" For example, under "Centrifuge not available," this question would lead to a deeper understanding of the problem such as "Rotor damaged," "Motor inoperable," and so on.

Tip For each deeper cause, continue to push for deeper understanding, but know when to stop. A rule of thumb is to stop questioning when a cause is controlled by more than one level of management removed from the group. Otherwise, the process could become an exercise in frustration. Use common sense.

e) Interpret or test for root cause(s) by one or more of the following:

- Look for causes that appear repeatedly within or across major cause categories.
- Select through either an unstructured consensus process or one that is structured, such as Nominal Group Technique or Multivoting.
- Gather data through Check Sheets or other formats to determine the relative frequencies of the different causes.

Variations

Traditionally, Cause & Effect Diagrams have been created in a meeting setting. The completed "fishbone" is often reviewed by others and/or confirmed with data collection. A very effective alternative is CEDAC®, in which a large, highly visible, blank fishbone chart is displayed prominently in a work area. Everyone posts both potential causes and solutions on sticky notes in each of the categories. Causes and solutions are reviewed, tested, and posted. This technique opens up the process to the knowledge and creativity of every person in the operation.

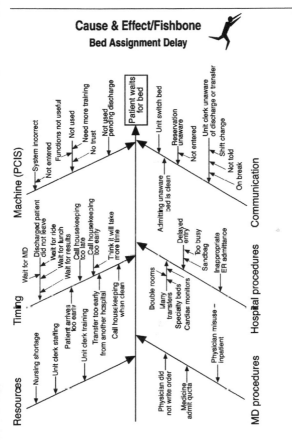

Cause & Effect/Fishbone
Bed Assignment Delay

Machine (PCIS)
- System incorrect
- Not entered
- Functions not useful
- Not used
- Need more training
- No trust
- Not used pending discharge

Communication
- Unit switch bed
- Reservation unaware
- Not entered
- Unit clerk unaware of discharge or transfer
- Shift change
- Not told
- On break

Timing
- Wait for MD
- Discharged patient did not leave
- Wait for ride
- Wait for lunch
- Patient arrives too early
- Wait for results
- Call housekeeping too late
- Call housekeeping too early
- Transfer too early from another hospital
- Think it will take more time
- Call housekeeping when clean

Hospital procedures
- Admitting unaware bed is clean
- Delayed entry
- Double rooms
- Many transfers
- Specialty beds
- Cardiac monitors
- Too busy
- Sandbag
- Inappropriate ER admittance

Resources
- Nursing shortage
- Unit clerk staffing
- Unit clerk training

MD procedures
- Physician did not write order
- Medicine admit quota
- Physician misuse – inpatient

Patient waits for bed

Information provided courtesy of
Rush-Presbyterian-St. Luke's Medical Center

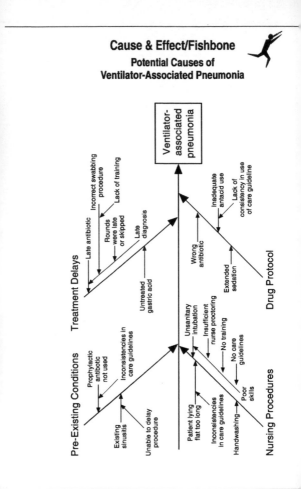

Cause & Effect/Fishbone

Potential Causes of Ventilator-Associated Pneumonia

Ventilator-associated pneumonia

Treatment Delays
- Late antibiotic
- Incorrect swabbing procedure
- Lack of training
- Rounds were late or skipped
- Late diagnosis
- Untreated gastric acid

Pre-Existing Conditions
- Prophylactic antibiotic not used
- Inconsistencies in care guidelines
- Existing sinusitis
- Unable to delay procedure

Drug Protocol
- Inadequate antacid use
- Lack of consistency in use of care guideline
- Wrong antibiotic
- Extended sedation

Nursing Procedures
- Unsanitary intubation
- Insufficient nurse proctoring
- No training
- No care guidelines
- Patient lying flat too long
- Inconsistencies in care guidelines
- Handwashing
- Poor skills

©1994, 2005, 2008 GOAL/QPC

Check Sheet
*Counting &
accumulating data*

	1	2	Total
A	▮	▮	7
B	▮	▮	7
C	▮	▮	3

Why use it?

To allow a team to systematically record and compile data from historical sources, or observations as they happen, so that patterns and trends can be clearly detected and shown.

What does it do?

- Creates easy-to-understand data that come from a simple, efficient process that can be applied to any key performance areas
- Builds, with each observation, a clearer picture of "the facts" as opposed to the opinions of each team member
- Forces agreement on the definition of each condition or event (every person has to be looking for and recording the same thing)
- Makes patterns in the data become obvious quickly

How do I do it?

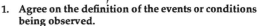

1. **Agree on the definition of the events or conditions being observed.**
    - If you are building a list of events or conditions as the observations are made, agree on the overall definition of the project.

    Example: If you are looking for reasons for admission delays, agree on the definition of "delays."

- If you are working from a standard list of events or conditions, make sure that there is agreement on the meaning and application of each one.

  Example: If you are tracking errors in various departments, make sure everyone knows which functions are in each department.

2. **Decide who will collect the data; over what period; and from what sources.**

- Who collects the data obviously depends on the project and resources. The data collection period can range from hours to months. The data can come from either a sample or an entire population.

- Make sure the data collector(s) have both the time and knowledge they need to collect accurate information.

- Collect the data over a sufficient period to be sure the data represents "typical" results during a "typical" cycle for your business.

- Sometimes there may be important differences within a population that should be reflected by sampling each different subgroup individually. This is called stratification.

  Example: Collect data for ventilator-associated pneumonia separately from other types of pneumonia. Collect data from each ventilator separately.

Tip It must be safe to record and report "bad news"; otherwise, the data will be filtered.

3. **Design a Check Sheet form that is clear, complete, and easy to use.**

• A complete Check Sheet, illustrated below, includes the following:

Source Information

a Name of project

b Location of data collection

c Name of person recording data, if it applies

d Date(s)

e Other important identifiers

Content Information

f Column with defect/event name

g Columns with collection days/dates

h Totals for each column

i Totals for each row

j Grand total for both the columns and rows

a Project: Admission Delays	c Name: (if applicable)							e Shift: All
b Location: Emergency Room	d Dates: 3/10 to 3/16							
f Reason:	g Date							i Total
	3/10	3/11	3/12	3/13	3/14	3/15	3/16	
Incomplete patient information	JHT IIII	IIII	JHT I	JHT I	III	JHT JHT II	JHT JHT II	52
No beds available	II	JHT II	II	IIII	JHT	JHT III	III	31
Lab delays	JHT II	III	I	II	II	IIII	JHT	24
h Total	33	28	36	30	25	47	38	j 237

Check Sheet 33

4. Collect the data consistently and accurately.

- Make sure all entries are written clearly.

Tip Managers and/or team members can do their part to help the data collector(s) do their job well by simply showing an interest in the project. Ask the collector(s) how the project is working out. Show your support—tell the data collector(s) you think it is important to collect the information. ***Above all—act on the data as quickly as possible!***

Variations

Defect Location

Shows the concentration of omissions by marking an "X" on a drawing of the object each time an omission is found.

```
Patient Name: _XX_____  DOB: _XXXX_____

Street Address: _X_____  SSN: _XXX_____

City: _____ State: _ Zip: _X_ Phone: _XXXX____

Requested Information:
  XXXX _____

  _____

  _____

Send To:
Name: _____
Address: _____
```

Task Checklist

Tasks in producing a product or delivering a service are checked off as they are done. In complex processes this is a form of "mistake proofing."

Check Sheet
Emergency Department Delays

Location: Emergency Department | **Name:** (if applicable) | **Shift:** All

Dates: 3/10 to 3/16

Reason:	3/10	3/11	3/12	3/13	3/14	3/15	3/16	Total
No wheelchair immediately available								7
Patient gets lost going to x-ray								11
Triage nurse not at triage desk								66
Phlebotomist not immediately available								42
MD must go to x-ray to review films with radiologist								21
ED room not yet cleaned, so patient can't be put in room								9
Nurses/MDs don't know which patients have been in ED for how long								35
Patient awaiting lab results that have to be sent to outside lab								11
Patient treated in ED rather than admitted								13
Patient awaiting admission to med/surg unit and bed not yet available								46
Other								10
Total	35	46	33	37	47	39	34	271

Information provided courtesy of Jim Salsbury

Control Charts
Recognizing sources of variation

Why use it?

To monitor, control, and improve process performance over time by studying variation and its source.

What does it do?

- Focuses attention on detecting and monitoring process variation over time
- Distinguishes special from common causes of variation, as a guide to local or management action
- Serves as a tool for ongoing control of a process
- Helps improve a process to perform consistently and predictably for higher quality, lower cost, and higher effective capacity
- Provides a common language for discussing process performance

How do I do it?

There are many types of Control Charts. The Control Chart(s) that your team decides to use will be determined by the type of data you have. Use the Tree Diagram on the next page to determine which Control Chart(s) will best fit your situation. Other types of Control Charts, which are beyond the scope of this book, include the Pre Control Chart, the Moving Average & Range Chart, the Cumulative Sum Chart, and Box Plots.

©1994, 2005, 2008 GOAL/QPC

Based on the type of data and sample size you have, choose the appropriate Control Chart.

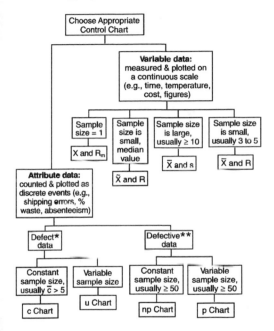

* Defect = Failure to meet one of the acceptance criteria.
  A defective unit might have multiple defects.

** Defective = An entire unit fails to meet acceptance
   criteria, regardless of the number of defects on the unit.

Constructing Control Charts

1. **Select the process to be charted.**

2. **Determine sampling method and plan.**
    - How large a sample can be drawn? Balance the time and cost to collect a sample with the amount of information you will gather. *See the Tree Diagram on the previous page for suggested sample sizes.*
    - As much as possible, obtain the samples under the same technical conditions: the same machine, operator, lot, and so on.
    - Frequency of sampling will depend on whether you are able to discern patterns in the data. Consider hourly, daily, shifts, monthly, annually, lots, and so on. Once the process is "in control," you might consider reducing the frequency with which you sample.
    - Generally, collect 20–25 groups of samples before calculating the statistics and control limits.
    - Consider using historical data to set a baseline.

    Tip Make sure samples are random. To establish the inherent variation of a process, allow the process to run untouched (i.e., according to standard procedures).

3. **Initiate data collection.**
    - Run the process untouched, and gather sampled data.
    - Record data on an appropriate Control Chart sheet or other graph paper. Include any unusual events that occur.

4. Calculate the appropriate statistics.

a) If you have attribute data, use the Attribute Data Table, Central Line column.

Attribute Data Table

Type Control Chart	Sample Size	Central Line	Control Limits
Fraction defective p Chart	Variable, usually ≥50	For each subgroup: $p = np/n$ For all subgroups: $\bar{p} = \Sigma np / \Sigma n$	$*UCL_p = \bar{p} + 3\sqrt{\dfrac{\bar{p}(1-\bar{p})}{n}}$ $*LCL_p = \bar{p} - 3\sqrt{\dfrac{\bar{p}(1-\bar{p})}{n}}$
Number defective np Chart	Constant, usually ≥50	For each subgroup: $np = \#$ defective units For all subgroups: $n\bar{p} = \Sigma np / k$	$UCL_{np} = n\bar{p} + 3\sqrt{n\bar{p}(1-\bar{p})}$ $LCL_{np} = n\bar{p} - 3\sqrt{n\bar{p}(1-\bar{p})}$
Number of defects c Chart	Constant	For each subgroup: $c = \#$ defects For all subgroups: $\bar{c} = \Sigma c / k$	$UCL_c = \bar{c} + 3\sqrt{\bar{c}}$ $LCL_c = \bar{c} - 3\sqrt{\bar{c}}$
Number of defects per unit u Chart	Variable	For each subgroup: $u = c/n$ For all subgroups: $\bar{u} = \Sigma c / \Sigma n$	$*UCL_u = \bar{u} + 3\sqrt{\dfrac{\bar{u}}{n}}$ $*LCL_u = \bar{u} - 3\sqrt{\dfrac{\bar{u}}{n}}$

$np = \#$ defective units
$c = \#$ of defects
$n =$ sample size within each subgroup
$k = \#$ of subgroups

* This formula creates changing control limits. To avoid this, use average sample sizes $\bar{n}$ for those samples that are within ±20% of the average sample size. Calculate individual limits for the samples exceeding ±20%.

b) If you have variable data, use the Variable Data Table, Central Line column.

Variable Data Table

Type Control Chart	Sample Size n	Central Line*	Control Limits
Average & Range	<10, but usually 3 to 5	$\bar{\bar{X}} = \dfrac{(\bar{X}_1 + \bar{X}_2 + ... \bar{X}_k)}{k}$	$UCL_{\bar{X}} = \bar{\bar{X}} + A_2\bar{R}$ $LCL_{\bar{X}} = \bar{\bar{X}} - A_2\bar{R}$
$\bar{X}$ and R		$\bar{R} = \dfrac{(R_1 + R_2 + ... R_k)}{k}$	$UCL_R = D_4\bar{R}$ $LCL_R = D_3\bar{R}$
Average & Standard Deviation	Usually ≥10	$\bar{\bar{X}} = \dfrac{(\bar{X}_1 + \bar{X}_2 + ... \bar{X}_k)}{k}$	$UCL_{\bar{X}} = \bar{\bar{X}} + A_3\bar{s}$ $LCL_{\bar{X}} = \bar{\bar{X}} - A_3\bar{s}$
$\bar{X}$ and s		$\bar{s} = \dfrac{(s_1 + s_2 + ... s_k)}{k}$	$UCL_s = B_4\bar{s}$ $LCL_s = B_3\bar{s}$
Median & Range	<10, but usually 3 or 5	$\bar{\tilde{X}} = \dfrac{(\tilde{X}_1 + \tilde{X}_2 + ... \tilde{X}_k)}{k}$	$UCL_{\tilde{X}} = \bar{\tilde{X}} + \tilde{A}_2\bar{R}$ $LCL_{\tilde{X}} = \bar{\tilde{X}} - \tilde{A}_2\bar{R}$
$\tilde{X}$ and R		$\bar{R} = \dfrac{(R_1 + R_2 + ... R_k)}{k}$	$UCL_R = D_4\bar{R}$ $LCL_R = D_3\bar{R}$
Individuals & Moving Range	1	$\bar{X} = \dfrac{(X_1 + X_2 + ... X_k)}{k}$	$UCL_X = \bar{X} + E_2\bar{R}_m$ $LCL_X = \bar{X} - E_2\bar{R}_m$
X and R_m		$R_m = |(X_{i+1} - X_i)|$ $\bar{R}_m = \dfrac{(R_1 + R_2 + ... R_{k-1})}{k-1}$	$UCL_{Rm} = D_4\bar{R}_m$ $LCL_{Rm} = D_3\bar{R}_m$

k = # of subgroups, $\tilde{X}$ = median value within each subgroup

*$\bar{X} = \dfrac{\Sigma X_i}{n}$

5. Calculate the control limits.

a) If you have attribute data, use the Attribute Data Table, Control Limits column.

b) If you have variable data, use the Variable Data Table, Control Limits column for the correct formula to use.

- Use the Table of Constants to match the numeric values to the constants in the formulas shown in the Control Limits column of the Variable Data Table. The values you will need to look up will depend on the type of Variable Control Chart you choose and on the size of the sample you have drawn.

Tip If the Lower Control Limit (LCL) of an Attribute Data Control Chart is a negative number, set the **LCL** to zero.

Tip The **p** and **u** formulas create changing control limits if the sample sizes vary subgroup to subgroup. To avoid this, use the average sample size, $\bar{n}$, for those samples that are within ±20% of the average sample size. Calculate individual limits for the samples exceeding ±20%.

6. Construct the Control Chart(s).

- For Attribute Data Control Charts, construct one chart, plotting each subgroup's proportion or number defective, number of defects, or defects per unit.

- For Variable Data Control Charts, construct two charts: on the top chart plot each subgroup's mean, median, or individuals, and on the bottom chart plot each subgroup's range or standard deviation.

Table of Constants

Sample Size n	$\bar{X}$ and R Chart			$\bar{X}$ and s Chart			
	A_2	D_3	D_4	A_3	B_3	B_4	c_4^*
2	1.880	0	3.267	2.659	0	3.267	.7979
3	1.023	0	2.574	1.954	0	2.568	.8862
4	0.729	0	2.282	1.628	0	2.266	.9213
5	0.577	0	2.114	1.427	0	2.089	.9400
6	0.483	0	2.004	1.287	0.030	1.970	.9515
7	0.419	0.076	1.924	1.182	0.118	1.882	.9594
8	0.373	0.136	1.864	1.099	0.185	1.815	.9650
9	0.337	0.184	1.816	1.032	0.239	1.761	.9693
10	0.308	0.223	1.777	0.975	0.284	1.716	.9727

Sample Size n	$\bar{X}$ and R Chart			X and R_m Chart			
	$\tilde{A}_2$	D_3	D_4	E_2	D_3	D_4	d_2^*
2	----	0	3.267	2.659	0	3.267	1.128
3	1.187	0	2.574	1.772	0	2.574	1.693
4	----	0	2.282	1.457	0	2.282	2.059
5	0.691	0	2.114	1.290	0	2.114	2.326
6	----	0	2.004	1.184	0	2.004	2.534
7	0.509	0.076	1.924	1.109	0.076	1.924	2.704
8	----	0.136	1.864	1.054	0.136	1.864	2.847
9	0.412	0.184	1.816	1.010	0.184	1.816	2.970
10	----	0.223	1.777	0.975	0.223	1.777	3.078

* Useful in estimating the process standard deviation $\hat{\sigma}$.

Note: The minimum sample size shown in this chart is 2 because variation in the form of a range can only be calculated in samples greater than 1. The X and R_m Chart creates these minimum samples by combining and then calculating the difference between sequential, individual measurements.

- Draw a solid horizontal line on each chart. This line corresponds to the process average.
- Draw dashed lines for the upper and lower control limits.

Interpreting Control Charts

- **Attribute Data Control Charts** are based on one chart. The charts for fraction or number defective, number of defects, or number of defects per unit, measure variation *between samples*. **Variable Data Control Charts** are based on two charts: the one on top, for averages, medians, and individuals, measures variation *between subgroups* over time; the chart below, for ranges and standard deviations, measures variation *within subgroups* over time.
- Determine if the process mean (center line) is where it should be relative to your customer specifications or your internal business needs or objectives. If not, then it is an indication that something has changed in the process, or the customer requirements or objectives have changed.
- Analyze the data relative to the control limits, distinguishing between *common* causes and *special* causes. The fluctuation of the points within the limits results from variation inherent in the process. This variation results from common causes within the system (e.g., design, choice of machine, preventive maintenance) and can only be affected by changing that system. However, points outside of the limits or patterns within the limits come from a special cause (e.g., human errors, unplanned events, freak occurrences) that is not part of the way the process normally operates, or is present because of an unlikely combination of process steps. Special causes must

be eliminated before the Control Chart can be used as a monitoring tool. Once this is done, the process will be "in control" and samples can be taken at regular intervals to make sure that the process doesn't fundamentally change. See "Determining if Your Process is Out of Control."

- Your process is in "statistical control" if the process is not being affected by special causes (i.e., the influence of an individual or machine). All the points must fall within the control limits and they must be randomly dispersed about the average line for an in-control system.

Tip "Control" doesn't necessarily mean that the product or service will meet your needs. It only means that the process is *consistent.* Don't confuse control limits with specification limits—specification limits are related to customer requirements, not process variation.

Tip Any points outside the control limits, once identified with a cause (or causes), should be removed and the calculations and charts redone. Points within the control limits, but showing indications of trends, shifts, or instability, are also special causes.

Tip When a Control Chart has been initiated and all special causes removed, continue to plot new data on a new chart, but DO NOT recalculate the control limits. As long as the process does not change, the limits should not be changed. Control limits should be recalculated only when a permanent, desired change has occurred in the process, and only using data *after* the change occurred.

Tip Nothing will change just because you charted it! You need to do something. Form a team to investigate. See "Common Questions for Investigating an Out-of-Control Process."

Determining if Your Process is "Out of Control"

A process is said to be "out of control" if either one of these is true:

1. One or more points fall outside of the control limits

2. When the Control Chart is divided into zones, as shown below, any of the following points are true:

a) Two points, out of three consecutive points, are on the same side of the average in Zone A or beyond.

b) Four points, out of five consecutive points, are on the same side of the average in Zone B or beyond.

c) Nine consecutive points are on one side of the average.

d) There are six consecutive points, increasing or decreasing.

e) There are fourteen consecutive points that alternate up and down.

f) There are fifteen consecutive points within Zone C (above and below the average).

Tests for Control

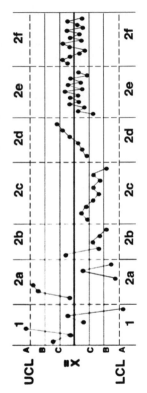

Source: Lloyd S. Nelson, Director of Statistical Methods, Nashua Corporation, New Hampshire

©1994, 2005, 2008 GOAL/QPC

Common Questions for Investigating
an Out-of-Control Process

❏ Yes ❏ No   Are there differences in the measurement accuracy of instruments/methods used?

❏ Yes ❏ No   Are there differences in the methods used by different personnel?

❏ Yes ❏ No   Is the process affected by the environment (e.g., temperature, humidity)?

❏ Yes ❏ No   Has there been a significant change in the environment?

❏ Yes ❏ No   Is the process affected by predictable conditions (e.g., tool wear)?

❏ Yes ❏ No   Were any untrained personnel involved in the process at the time?

❏ Yes ❏ No   Has there been a change in the source for input to the process (e.g., raw materials, information)?

❏ Yes ❏ No   Is the process affected by employee fatigue?

❏ Yes ❏ No   Has there been a change in policies or procedures (e.g., maintenance procedures)?

❏ Yes ❏ No   Is the process adjusted frequently?

❏ Yes ❏ No   Did the samples come from different parts of the process? Shifts? Individuals?

❏ Yes ❏ No   Are employees afraid to report "bad news"?

A team should address each "Yes" answer as a potential source of a special cause.

Individuals & Moving Range Chart

IV Lines Connection Time

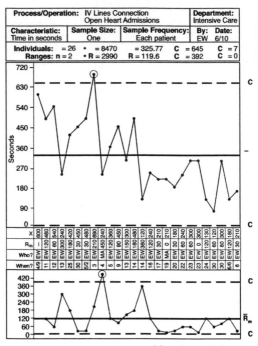

Process/Operation:	IV Lines Connection Open Heart Admissions		Department: Intensive Care	
Characteristic: Time in seconds	**Sample Size:** One	**Sample Frequency:** Each patient	**By:** EW	**Date:** 6/10
Individuals: = 26	• = 8470	= 325.77	**C** = 645	**C** = 7
Ranges: n = 2	• **R** = 2990	R = 119.6	**C** = 392	**C** = 0

Information provided courtesy of Parkview Episcopal Medical Center

Note: Something in the process changed, and now it takes less time to make IV connections for patients being admitted for open heart surgery.

©1994, 2005, 2008 GOAL/QPC

p Chart

General Dentistry: Percent of
Patients Who Failed to Keep Appointments

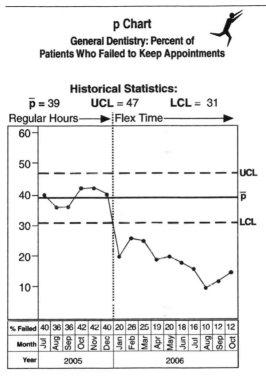

Historical Statistics:

$\bar{p}$ = 39   UCL = 47   LCL = 31

Regular Hours ➤ Flex Time ➤

% Failed	40	36	36	42	42	40	20	26	25	19	20	18	16	10	12	12
Month	Jul	Aug	Sep	Oct	Nov	Dec	Jan	Feb	Mar	Apr	May	Jun	Jul	Aug	Sep	Oct
Year	2005						2006									

*Adapted from information provided courtesy of U.S. Navy,
Naval Dental Center, San Diego*

Note: Providing flex time for patients resulted in fewer appointments missed.

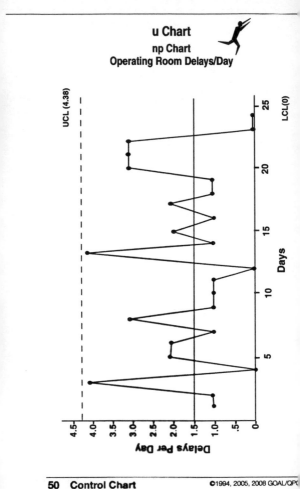

u Chart

np Chart
Operating Room Delays/Day

©1994, 2005, 2008 GOAL/QPC

$\overline{X}$ & R Chart

High Usage
Immunization Clinic Data

Measurement: Wait times of clients (in minutes)
vs. efficient utilization of nursing staff

n = 5 samples taken randomly 4 times a day for 1 week

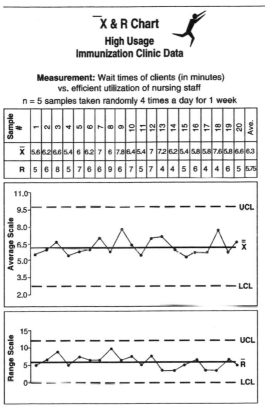

Sample #	1	2	3	4	5	6	7	8	9	10	11	12	13	14	15	16	17	18	19	20	Ave.
$\overline{X}$	5.6	6.2	6.6	5.4	6	6.2	7	6	7.8	6.4	5.4	7	7.2	6.2	5.4	5.8	5.8	7.6	5.8	6.6	6.3
R	5	6	8	5	7	6	6	9	6	7	5	7	4	4	5	6	4	4	6	5	5.75

Information provided courtesy of Nicholas Governale

Note: Based on the data above, the team decided that although nurse utilization was not a factor, client waiting time was trending on the high side and needed to be addressed.

Data Points
*Turning data
into information*

What Type of Data Do You Have?

- Words?
- Numbers?
  - *Attribute data?* Attribute data can be counted and plotted as discrete events. It includes the count of the numbers or percentages of good or bad, right or wrong, pass or fail, yes or no.

    Example: Number of correct answers on a test, number of mistakes per typed page, percent defective product per shift.

  - *Variable data?* Variable data can be measured and plotted on a continuous scale.

    Example: Length, time, volume, weight.

Do You Need to Collect Data?

- If you need to know the performance of an entire population, the more economical and less time-consuming method is to draw a sample from a population. With a sample, you can make inferences about, or predict, the performance of a population. Basic sampling methods:
  - *Random.* Each and every observation or data measure has an equally likely chance of being selected. Use a random number table or random number generator to select the samples.
  - *Sequential.* Every *nth* sample is selected.
  - *Stratified.* A sample is taken from stratified data groups.

Can You Categorize Your Data Into Subgroups?

- When you stratify data, you break it down into meaningful subcategories or classifications, and from this point you can focus your problem solving.

  Example: Data often comes from many sources but is treated as if coming from one. Data on nosocomial infections may be recorded as a single figure, but that number could actually be the sum total of infections by 1) type, 2) location, and 3) department. Below is an example of how data has been stratified by type.

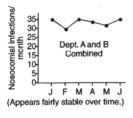

(Appears fairly stable over time.)

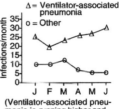

(Ventilator-associated pneumonia is running higher and may be increasing over time.)

What Patterns are Important in Your Data?

Predictable patterns or distributions can be described with statistics.

- **Measures of location**
  - *Mean* (or average). Represented by $\bar{X}$ (or **X**-bar), the mean is the sum of the values of the sample $(X_1, X_2, X_3 \ldots X_n)$ divided by the total number **(n)** of sampled data.

    Example: For the sample: (3, 5, 4, 7, 5)

    $$\bar{X} = \frac{(3 + 5 + 4 + 7 + 5)}{5} = 4.8$$

- *Median.* When sampled data are rank ordered, lowest to highest, the median is the middle number.

  Example: For the sample: (3, 5, 4, 7, 5)
  Median of (3, 4, 5, 5, 7) = 5

  When there are an even number of values, the median is the average of the middle two values.

  Example: For the sample: (2, 5, 7, 4, 5, 3)
  Median of (2, 3, 4, 5, 5, 7) = 4.5

- *Mode.* The most frequently occurring value(s) in a sample.

  Example: For the sample: (3, 5, 4, 7, 5)
  Mode = 5

- **Measures of variation**
  - *Range.* Represented by R, the range is the difference between the highest data value (X_{max}) and the lowest data value (X_{min}).

    Example: For the sample: (3, 5, 4, 7, 5)
    $R = 7 - 3 = 4$

  - *Standard Deviation.* Represented by **s**, the standard deviation of a sample measures the varia-tion of the data around the mean. The less variation there is of the data values about the mean, $\overline{X}$, the closer **s** will be to zero (0).

©1994, 2005, 2008 GOAL/QPC

Example: For the sample: (3, 5, 4, 7, 5) $\bar{X} = 4.8$

$$s = \sqrt{\frac{[(3-4.8)^2 + (5-4.8)^2 + (4-4.8)^2 + (7-4.8)^2 + (5-4.8)^2]}{5-1}}$$

$$= \sqrt{\frac{[3.24 + .04 + .64 + 4.84 + .04]}{4}}$$

$$= \sqrt{\frac{8.8}{4}}$$

$$= \sqrt{2.2}$$

$$= 1.48$$

The square of the standard deviation, **s**, is referred to as the *variance*. Variance is not discussed in this book.

Flowchart
*Picturing
the process*

Why use it?

To allow a team to identify the actual flow or sequence of events in a process that any product or service follows. Flowcharts can be applied to anything from the travels of records or the flow of materials, to the steps in preparing for surgery or admitting a patient.

What does it do?

- Shows unexpected complexity, problem areas, redundancy, unnecessary loops, and where simplification and standardization may be possible
- Compares and contrasts the actual versus the ideal flow of a process to identify improvement opportunities
- Allows a team to come to agreement on the steps of the process and to examine which activities may impact the process performance
- Identifies locations where additional data can be collected and investigated
- Serves as a training aid to understand the complete process

How do I do it?

1. **Determine the frame or boundaries of the process.**
   - Clearly define where the process under study starts (input) and ends (final output).
   - Team members should agree on the level of detail they must show on the Flowchart to clearly understand the process and identify problem areas.

- The Flowchart can be a simple macro flowchart showing only sufficient information to understand the general process flow, or it might be detailed to show every finite action and decision point. The team might start out with a macro flowchart and then add in detail later or only where it is needed.

2. Determine the steps in the process.

- Brainstorm a list of all major activities, inputs, outputs, and decisions on a flipchart sheet from the beginning of the process to the end.

3. Sequence the steps.

- Arrange the steps in the order they are carried out. Use sticky notes so you can move them around. Don't draw in the arrows yet.

Tip Unless you are flowcharting a new process, sequence what *is*, not what *should be* or the ideal. This may be difficult at first but is necessary to see where the probable causes of the problems are in the process.

4. Draw the Flowchart using the appropriate symbols.

An oval is used to show the materials, information, or action (inputs) to start the process or to show the results at the end (output) of the process.

A box or rectangle is used to show a task or activity performed in the process. Although multiple arrows may come into each box, usually only one output or arrow leaves each activity box.

$\diamondsuit$ A diamond shows those points in the process where a yes/no question is being asked or a decision is required.

$\left(\text{A}\right)$ A circle with either a letter or a number identifies a break in the Flowchart and is continued elsewhere on the same page or another page.

$\longrightarrow$ Arrows show the direction or flow of the process.

- Keep the Flowchart simple using the basic symbols listed above. As your experience grows, use other, more graphic symbols to represent the steps. Other symbols sometimes used include:
  - A half or torn sheet of paper for a report completed and/or filed
  - A can or computer tape wheel for data entry into a computer database
  - A large "D" or half circle to identify places in the process where there is a delay or wait for further action
- Be consistent in the level of detail shown.
  - A macro-level flowchart will show key action steps but no decision boxes.
  - An intermediate-level flowchart will show action and decision points.
  - A micro-level flowchart will show minute detail.
- Label each process step using words that are understandable to everyone.
- Add arrows to show the direction of the flow of steps in the process. Although not a rule, if you show all "yes" choices branching down and "no" choices branching to the left, it is easier to follow

©1994, 2005, 2008 GOAL/QPC

the process. Preferences and space will later dictate direction.

- Don't forget to identify your work. Include the title of your process, the date the diagram was made, and the names of the team members.

5. Test the Flowchart for completeness.

- Are the symbols used correctly?
- Are the process steps (inputs, outputs, actions, decisions, waits/delays) identified clearly?
- Make sure every feedback loop is closed (i.e., every path takes you either back to or ahead to another step).
- Check that every continuation point has a corresponding point elsewhere in the Flowchart or on another page of the Flowchart.
- There is usually only one output arrow out of an activity box. If there is more than one arrow, you may need a decision diamond.
- Validate the Flowchart with people who are not on the team and who carry out the process actions. Highlight additions or deletions they recommend. Bring these back to the team to discuss and incorporate into the final Flowchart.

6. Finalize the Flowchart.

- Is this process being run the way it should be?
- Are people following the process as charted?
- Are there obvious complexities or redundancies that can be reduced or eliminated?
- How different is the current process from an ideal one? Draw an ideal Flowchart. Compare the two (current versus ideal) to identify discrepancies and opportunities for improvements.

Variations

The type of Flowchart just described is sometimes referred to as a "detailed" flowchart because it includes, in detail, the inputs, activities, decision points, and outputs of any process. Four other forms, described below, are also useful.

Macro Flowchart

Refer to the third bulleted item in Step 1 of this section for a description. For a graphic example, see Step 2 of the Improvement Storyboard in the Problem-Solving/Process Improvement Model section.

Top-down Flowchart

This chart is a picture of the major steps in a work process. It minimizes the detail to focus only on those steps essential to the process. It usually does not include inspection, rework, and other steps that result in quality problems. Teams sometimes study the top-down flowchart to look for ways to simplify or reduce the number of steps to make the process more efficient and effective.

Universal Precautions Training for Nonmedical (Custodial) Staff

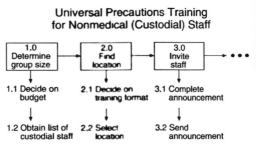

Deployment Flowchart

This chart shows the people or departments responsible and the flow of the process steps or tasks they are assigned. It is useful to clarify roles and track accountability as well as to indicate dependencies in the sequence of events.

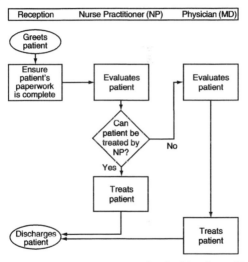

Based on information provided courtesy of Jim Salsbury

Workflow Flowchart

This type of chart is used to show the flow of people, materials, paperwork, etc., within a work setting. When redundancies, duplications, and unnecessary complexities are identified in a path, people can take action to reduce or eliminate these problems.

Flowchart
Suggestion For Improvement

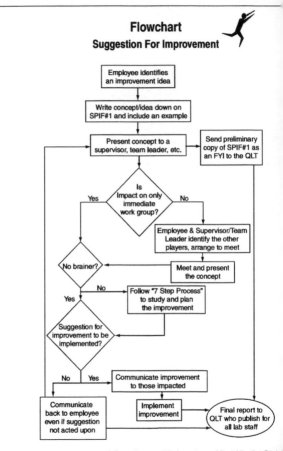

Information provided courtesy of Park Nicollet Clinic HealthSystems Minnesota, Minneapolis, Minnesota

©1994, 2005, 2008 GOAL/QPC

Force Field Analysis
Positives & negatives of change

Why use it?

To identify the forces and factors in place that support or work against the solution of an issue or problem so that the positives can be reinforced and/or the negatives eliminated or reduced.

What does it do?

- Presents the "positives" and "negatives" of a situation so they are easily compared
- Forces people to think together about all the aspects of making the desired change a permanent one
- Encourages people to agree about the relative priority of factors on each side of the "balance sheet"
- Encourages honest reflection on the real underlying roots of a problem and its solution

How do I do it?

1. **Draw a large letter "T" on a flipchart.**

   a) At the top of the T, write the issue or problem that you plan to analyze.

   - To the far right of the top of the T, write a description of the ideal situation you would like to achieve.

   b) Brainstorm the forces that are driving you toward the ideal situation. These forces may be internal or external. List them on the left side.

c) Brainstorm the forces that are restraining movement toward the ideal state. List them on the right side.

2. **Prioritize the driving forces that can be strengthened or identify restraining forces that would allow the most movement toward the ideal state if they were removed.**

   - Achieve consensus through discussion or by using ranking methods such as Nominal Group Technique and Multivoting.

   Tip When choosing a target for change, remember that simply pushing the positive factors for a change can have the opposite effect. It is often more helpful to remove barriers. This tends to break the "change bottleneck" rather than just pushing on all the good reasons to change.

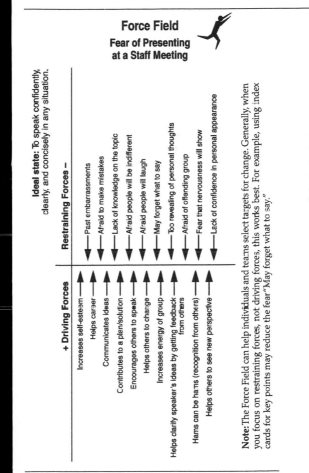

Force Field
Fear of Presenting at a Staff Meeting

Ideal state: To speak confidently, clearly, and concisely in any situation.

+ Driving Forces	Restraining Forces –
Increases self-esteem	Past embarrassments
Helps career	Afraid to make mistakes
Communicates ideas	Lack of knowledge on the topic
Contributes to a plan/solution	Afraid people will be indifferent
Encourages others to speak	Afraid people will laugh
Helps others to change	May forget what to say
Increases energy of group	Too revealing of personal thoughts
Helps clarify speaker's ideas by getting feedback from others	Afraid of offending group
Harns can be harns (recognition from others)	Fear that nervousness will show
Helps others to see new perspective	Lack of confidence in personal appearance

Note: The Force Field can help individuals and teams select targets for change. Generally, when you focus on restraining forces, not driving forces, this works best. For example, using index cards for key points may reduce the fear "May forget what to say."

2. Gather data.

- Collect at least 50 to 100 data points if you plan on looking for patterns and calculating the distribution's centering (mean), spread (variation), and shape. You might also consider collecting data for a specified period of time: hour, shift, day, week, etc.

- Use historical data to find patterns or to use as a baseline measure of past performance.

3. Prepare a frequency table from the data.

a) Count the number of data points, **n**, in the sample.

9.9	9.3	10.2	9.4	10.1	9.6	9.9	10.1	9.8
9.8	9.8	10.1	9.9	9.7	9.8	9.9	10.0	9.6
9.7	9.4	9.6	10.0	9.8	9.9	10.1	10.4	10.0
10.2	10.1	9.8	10.1	10.3	10.0	10.2	9.8	10.7
9.9	10.7	9.3	10.3	9.9	9.8	10.3	9.5	9.9
9.3	10.2	9.2	9.9	9.7	9.9	9.8	9.5	9.4
9.0	9.5	9.7	9.7	9.8	9.8	9.3	9.6	9.7
10.0	9.7	9.4	9.8	9.4	9.6	10.0	10.3	9.8
9.5	9.7	10.6	9.5	10.1	10.0	9.8	10.1	9.6
9.6	9.4	10.1	9.5	10.1	10.2	9.8	9.5	9.3
10.3	9.6	9.7	9.7	10.1	9.8	9.7	10.0	10.0
9.5	9.5	9.8	9.9	9.2	10.0	10.0	9.7	9.7
9.9	10.4	9.3	9.6	10.2	9.7	9.7	9.7	10.7
9.9	10.2	9.8	9.3	9.6	9.5	9.6	10.7	

In this example, there are 125 data points (**n** = 125).

b) Determine the range, **R**, for the entire sample.

The range is the smallest value in the set of data subtracted from the largest value. For our example:

$$R = X_{max} - X_{min} = 10.7 - 9.0 = 1.7$$

c) Determine the number of class intervals, **k**, needed.

- Use the smallest individual meas

5. Interpret the Histogram.

a) *Centering.* Where is the distribution centered? the process running too high? Too low?

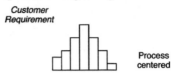

Customer
Requirement

Process
centered

Process
too high

Process
too low

5. **Interpret the Histogram.**

a) *Centering.* Where is the distribution centered? Is the process running too high? Too low?

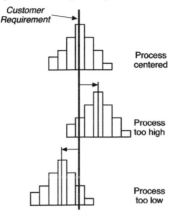

b) *Variation.* What is the variation or spread of the data? Is it too variable?

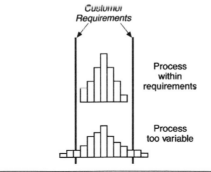

Tip Get suspicious of the accuracy of the data if ▮
Histogram suddenly stops at one point (such a
specification limit) without some previous

Centering and Spread Compared to Customer Target and Limits

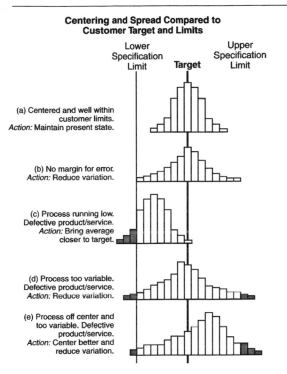

Lower Specification Limit **Target** **Upper Specification Limit**

(a) Centered and well within customer limits.
Action: Maintain present state.

(b) No margin for error.
Action: Reduce variation.

(c) Process running low. Defective product/service.
Action: Bring average closer to target.

(d) Process too variable. Defective product/service.
Action: Reduce variation.

(e) Process off center and too variable. Defective product/service.
Action: Center better and reduce variation.

Tip Get suspicious of the accuracy of the data if the Histogram suddenly stops at one point (such as a specification limit) without some previous de-cline in the data. It could indicate that defective product is being sorted out and is not included in the sample.

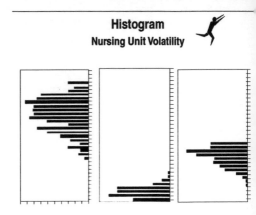

All Nursing Units

cal issues so that key drivers or outcomes can become the heart of an effective solution.

What does it do?

- Encourages team members to think in multiple directions rather than linearly
- Explores the cause and effect relationships among all the issues, including the most controversial
- Allows the key issues to emerge naturally rather than allowing the issues to be forced by a dominant or powerful team member
- Systematically surfaces the basic assumptions and reasons for disagreements among team members
- Allows a team to identify root cause(s) even when credible data doesn't exist

How do I do it?

1. **Agree on the issue/problem statement.**

> **What are the issues related to regulated medical waste (RMW) reduction?**

- If using an original statement (it didn't come from a previous tool or discussion), create a complete sentence that is clearly understood and agreed on by team members.

- If using input from other tools (such as an Affinity Diagram), make sure that the goal under discussion is still the same and clearly understood.

2. Assemble the right team.

- The ID requires more intimate knowledge of the subject under discussion than is needed for the Affinity. This is important if the final cause and effect patterns are to be credible.

- The ideal team size is generally 4–6 people. However, this number can be increased as long as the issues are still visible and the meeting is well facilitated to encourage participation and maintain focus.

3. Lay out all of the ideas/issue cards that have either been brought from other tools or brainstormed.

- Arrange 5–25 cards or notes in a large circular pattern, leaving as much space as possible for drawing arrows. Use large, bold printing, including a large number or letter on each idea for quick reference later in the process.

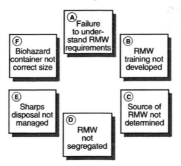

4. Look for cause/influence relationships between all of the ideas and draw relationship arrows.

- Choose any of the ideas as a starting point. If all of the ideas are numbered or lettered, work through them in sequence.
- An outgoing arrow from an idea indicates that it is the stronger cause or influence.

Ask of each combination:
1) Is there a cause/influence relationship?
2) If yes, which direction of cause/influence is stronger?

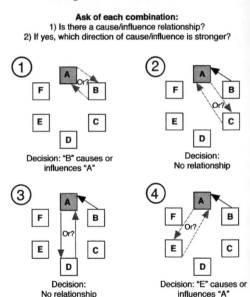

Decision: "B" causes or influences "A"

Decision: No relationship

Decision: No relationship

Decision: "E" causes or influences "A"

Continued on next page

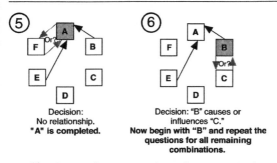

Decision:
No relationship.
"A" is completed.

Decision: "B" causes or
influences "C."
**Now begin with "B" and repeat the
questions for all remaining
combinations.**

Tip Draw only one-way relationship arrows in the
direction of the stronger cause or influence. Make
a decision on the stronger direction. ***Do not draw
two-headed arrows.***

5. **Review and revise the first-round ID.**

   • Get additional input from people who are not on
   the team to confirm or modify the team's work.
   Either bring the paper version to others or repro-
   duce it using available software. Use a different
   size print or a color marker to make additions or
   deletions.

6. **Tally the number of outgoing and incoming arrows
   and select key items for further planning.**

   • Record and clearly mark next to each issue the
   number of arrows going in and out of it.

   • Find the item(s) with the highest number of *outgoing arrows* and the item(s) with the highest number of *incoming arrows*.

   • *Outgoing arrows.* A high number of outgoing arrows
   indicates an item that is a root cause or driver. This is
   generally the issue that teams tackle first.

- *Incoming arrows.* A high number of incoming arrows indicates an item that is a key outcome. This can become a focus for planning either as a meaningful measure of overall success or as a redefinition of the original issue under discussion.

Tip Use common sense when you select the most-critical issues to focus on. Issues with very close tallies must be reviewed carefully, but in the end, it is a judgment call, not science.

7. Draw the final ID.

- Identify visually both the *key drivers* (greatest number of outgoing arrows) and the *key outcomes* (greatest number of incoming arrows). Typical methods are double boxes or bold boxes.

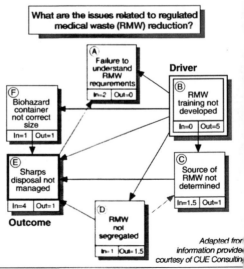

What are the issues related to regulated medical waste (RMW) reduction?

Ⓐ Failure to understand RMW requirements — In=2 | Out=0

Driver

Ⓑ RMW training not developed — In=0 | Out=5

Ⓕ Biohazard container not correct size — In=1 | Out=1

Ⓔ Sharps disposal not managed — In=4 | Out=1

Outcome

Ⓒ Source of RMW not determined — In=1.5 | Out=1

Ⓓ RMW not segregated — In=1 | Out=1.5

Adapted from information provided courtesy of CUE Consulting

Variations

When it is necessary to create a more orderly display of all of the relationships, a matrix format is very effective. The vertical (up) arrow is a driving cause and the horizontal (side) arrow is an effect. The example below has added symbols indicating the strength of the relationships.

The "total" column is the sum of all of the "relationship strengths" in each row. This shows that you are working on those items that have the strongest effect on the greatest number of issues.

ID – Matrix Format

	Logistic Support	Customer Satisfaction	Education & Training	Personnel Incentives	Leadership	Cause/ Driver ⬆	Result/ Rider ⬅	Total
Logistic Support		◉ ⬅	◯ ⬆	△ ⬅	◯ ⬅	3	1	16
Customer Satisfaction	◉ ⬅		◯ ⬅	◉ ⬅	◯ ⬅	0	4	24
Education & Training	◯ ⬅	◯ ⬅		◯ ⬆	◉ ⬅	2	2	18
Personnel Incentives	△ ⬅	◉ ⬅	◯ ⬅		◉ ⬅	1	3	22
Leadership	◯ ⬆	◯ ⬆	◉ ⬆	◉ ⬆		4	0	24

Relationship Strength

◉ = 9 Significant
◯ = 3 Medium
△ = 1 Weak

Information provided courtesy of U.S. Air Force, Air Combat Command

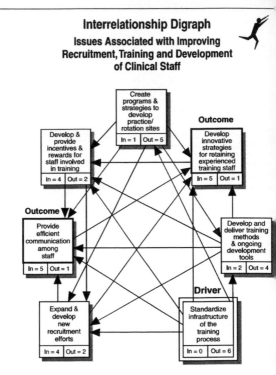

Interrelationship Digraph

Issues Associated with Improving Recruitment, Training and Development of Clinical Staff

Create programs & strategies to develop practice/rotation sites
In = 1 Out = 5

Outcome

Develop innovative strategies for retaining experienced training staff
In = 5 Out = 1

Develop & provide incentives & rewards for staff involved in training
In = 4 Out = 2

Outcome

Provide efficient communication among staff
In = 5 Out = 1

Develop and deliver training methods & ongoing development tools
In = 2 Out = 4

Expand & develop new recruitment efforts
In = 4 Out = 2

Driver

Standardize infrastructure of the training process
In = 0 Out = 6

Adapted from information provided courtesy of The American Association of Colleges of Pharmacy

Note: "The drivers" from an ID can be used as the goal in a Tree Diagram.

Interrelationship Digraph
Educational Change

Problem: How do we ensure that regulations & accreditation standards promote rigorous accountability & provide incentives for improvements in patient-centered care?

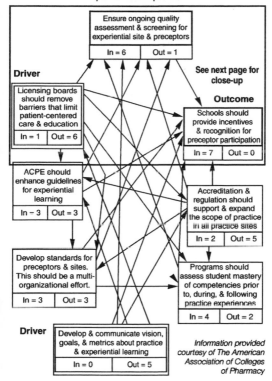

Ensure ongoing quality assessment & screening for experiential site & preceptors

| In = 6 | Out = 1 |

Driver

See next page for close-up

Licensing boards should remove barriers that limit patient-centered care & education

| In = 1 | Out = 6 |

Outcome

Schools should provide incentives & recognition for preceptor participation

| In = 7 | Out = 0 |

ACPE should enhance guidelines for experiential learning

| In = 3 | Out = 3 |

Accreditation & regulation should support & expand the scope of practice in all practice sites

| In = 2 | Out = 5 |

Develop standards for preceptors & sites. This should be a multi-organizational effort.

| In = 3 | Out = 3 |

Programs should assess student mastery of competencies prior to, during, & following practice experiences

| In = 4 | Out = 2 |

Driver

Develop & communicate vision, goals, & metrics about practice & experiential learning

| In = 0 | Out = 5 |

Information provided courtesy of The American Association of Colleges of Pharmacy

Close-up

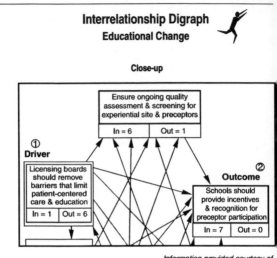

Ensure ongoing quality assessment & screening for experiential site & preceptors

| In = 6 | Out = 1 |

① **Driver**

Licensing boards should remove barriers that limit patient-centered care & education

| In = 1 | Out = 6 |

② **Outcome**

Schools should provide incentives & recognition for preceptor participation

| In = 7 | Out = 0 |

Information provided courtesy of
The American Association of Colleges of Pharmacy

① This is the driver. If the focus is on removing the barriers, then the outcome should be plentiful.

② This is the primary outcome. It puts incentives and recognition as a key indicator of the vision working.

Matrix Diagram
Finding relationships

	a	b	c
1			
2			
3			

Why use it?

To allow a team or individual to systematically identify, analyze, and rate the presence and strength of relationships between two or more sets of information.

What does it do?

- Makes patterns of responsibilities visible and clear so that there is an even and appropriate distribution of tasks
- Helps a team get consensus on small decisions, enhancing the quality and support for the final decision
- Improves a team's discipline in systematically taking a hard look at a large number of important decision factors

Types of Matrices

Most Common

- *L-shaped matrix.* Two sets of items directly compared to each other or a single set compared to itself.

Orienting New Staff

Tasks / Resources	Tour facility	Review personnel & safety policies	Review business values	Introduce to team members
Human resources		◯	△	
Division manager			⊙	
Supervisor	△	⊙	◯	◯
Associates	⊙	△	△	⊙

⊙ Primary responsibility
◯ Team members
△ Resources

Conclusion: Supervisors and associates have taken on the orientation role rather than the traditional human resource function.

©1994, 2005, 2008 GOAL/QPC

- *T-shaped matrix.* Two sets of items compared to a common third set.

Orienting New Staff

	Tour facility	Review personnel & safety policies	Review business values	Introduce to team members
Communicate organization spirit	●	○	●	●
Communicate purpose of organization			●	●
Resolve practical concerns	●	●	○	●
Reduce anxiety	●	●	●	●
Goals — Tasks / Resources	Tour facility	Review personnel & safety policies	Review business values	Introduce to team members
Human resources		○	△	
Division manager			●	
Supervisor	△	●	○	○
Associates	●	△	△	●

Responsibility
● Primary
○ Team members
△ Resources

Impact
● High
○ Medium
△ Low

Conclusion: The most important purpose of orientation is to reduce anxiety, and the most effective tasks focus on the personal issues.

Uncommon

- *Y-shaped matrix.* Three sets of items compared to each other. It "bends" a T-shaped matrix to allow comparisons between items that are on the vertical axes.

Rarely Used

- *X-shaped matrix.* Four sets of items compared to each other. It is essentially two T-shaped matrices placed back to back.

- *C-shaped matrix.* Shows the intersection of three sets of data simultaneously. It is a three-dimensional graphic.
- You can find more complete information on the Y-, X-, and C-shaped matrix in *The Memory Jogger Plus+®*.

How do I do it?

1. **Select the key factors affecting successful implementation.**
   - The most important step is to choose the issues or factors to be compared. The format is secondary. Begin with the right issues and the best format will define itself. The most common use is the distribution of responsibilities within an L-shaped or T-shaped matrix.

2. **Assemble the right team.**
   - Select individuals that have the influence/power to realistically assess the chosen factors.
   - *Tip* When distributing responsibilities, include those people who will likely be involved in the assigned tasks or who can at least be part of a review team to confirm small group results.

3. **Select an appropriate matrix format.**
   - Base your choice of format on the number of sets of items and types of comparisons you need to make.

4. **Choose and define relationship symbols.**
   - The most common symbols in matrix analysis are ⊙, ○, △. Generally they are used to indicate:
⊙	=	High	= 9
○	=	Medium	= 3
△	=	Low	= 1

- The possible meanings of the symbols are almost endless. The only requirement is that the team comes to a clear understanding and creates an equally clear legend with the matrix.

5. **Complete the matrix.**
   - If distributing responsibilities, use only one "primary responsibility" symbol to show ultimate accountability. All core team members can be given secondary responsibilities.

   Tip Focus the quality of the decision in each matrix cell. Do not try to "stack the deck" by consciously building a pattern of decisions. Let these patterns emerge naturally.

   Tip Interpret the matrix using total numerical values only when it adds value. Often the visual pattern is sufficient to interpret the overall results.

Variations

The matrix is one of the most versatile tools available. The important skill to master is "matrix thinking." This approach allows a team to focus its discussion on related factors that are explored thoroughly. The separate conclusions are then brought together to create high-quality decisions. Use your creativity in determining which factors affect each other, and in choosing the matrix format that will help focus the discussion toward the ultimate decision.

Matrix

Educating MD Residents
About Birth Center Protocols

Objectives / Resources	Hospital safety & policies	Department-specific policies	IT orientation	Role-specific responsibilities
Attending MD				◯
Departmental Director	◯	◉	△	◉
Nurse		◯		
Associates		◯		◯
Human Resources	◉	△	◉	

◉ = Primary responsibility

◯ = Secondary responsibility

△ = Kept informed

Information provided courtesy of Natalie Twaddel, RN, BSN, RNC

Matrix
Critical Roles in Training

Personnel	Infection control inspection	Ventilator care chart development	Clinical training	Data monitoring	Coordination of medical staff
Clark, Admin	○		△	⊙	
Foley, NP	⊙	○		○	
Wells, MD	△		⊙		⊙
Hering, HR			○		
Cho, MD	△	⊙			

Metrics / Tasks	Infection control inspection	Ventilator care chart development	Clinical training	Data monitoring	Coordination of medical staff
Staff training $	○		⊙	△	
Time on ventilator		⊙			○
Infection rates	⊙			○	△

Responsibility

⊙ = Primary

○ = Secondary

△ = Kept informed

Impact

⊙ = Strong influence

○ = Some influence

△ = Weak influence

Information provided courtesy of
Lisa Boisvert, Business Centered Learning, LLC

Nominal Group Technique (NGT)
Ranking for consensus

A. 2+2
B. 1+1
C. 3+4
D. 4+3

Why use it?

Allows a team to quickly come to a consensus on the relative importance of issues, problems, or solutions by completing individual importance rankings into a team's final priorities.

What does it do?

- Builds commitment to the team's choice through equal participation in the process
- Allows every team member to rank issues without being pressured by others
- Puts quiet team members on an equal footing with more dominant members
- Makes a team's consensus (or lack of it) visible; the major causes of disagreement can be discussed

How do I do it?

1. **Generate the list of issues, problems, or solutions to be prioritized.**
   - In a new team with members who are not accustomed to team participation, it may feel safer to do written, silent brainstorming, especially when dealing with sensitive topics.

2. **Write statements on a flipchart or board.**

3. **Eliminate duplicates and/or clarify meanings of any of the statements.**

   - As a leader, *always* ask for the team's permission and guidance when changing statements.

4. **Record the final list of statements on a flipchart or board.**

   Example: Why are there inconsistencies in depart-mental error reports?

A	Lack of training
B	No documented process
C	Unclear quality standards
D	Lack of communication among staff
E	High turnover

   - Use letters rather than numbers to identify each statement so that team members do not get con-fused by the ranking process that follows.

5. **Each team member records the corresponding letters on a piece of paper and rank orders the statements.**

   Example: Larry's sheet of paper looks like this:

A	4
B	5
C	3
D	1
E	2

   - This example uses "5" as the most important ranking and "1" as the least important. Because individual rankings will later be combined, this "reverse order" minimizes the effect of team members leaving some statements blank. Therefore, a blank (value = 0) would not, in effect, increase its importance.

6. Combine the rankings of all team members.

	Larry	Nina	Norm	Paige	Si		Total
A	4	5	2	2	1	=	14
B	5	4	5	3	5	=	22
C	3	1	3	4	4	=	15
D	1	2	1	5	2	=	11
E	2	3	4	1	3	=	13

"No documented process," B, would be the highest priority. The team would work on this first and then move through the rest of the list as needed.

Variations

One Half Plus One

When dealing with a large number of choices it may be necessary to limit the number of items ranked. The "one half plus one" approach would rank only a portion of the total. For example, if 20 ideas were generated, then team members would rank only the top 11 choices. If needed, this process could be repeated with the remaining 9 items, ranking the top 5 or 6 items, (half of 9 = 4.5 + 1 = 5.5), until a manageable number are identified.

Weighted Multivoting

Each team member *rates, not ranks,* the relative importance of choices by distributing a value (e.g., 100 points) across the options. Each team member can distribute this value among as many or as few choices as desired.

Example:

	Larry	Nina	Norm	Paige	Si		Total
A	20		10			=	30
B	40	80	50	100	45	=	315
C	30	5	10		25	=	70
D		5	10		20	=	35
E	10	10	20		10	=	50

With large numbers of choices, or when the voting for the top choices is very close, this process can be repeated for an agreed-upon number of items. Stop when the choice is clear.

Pareto Chart
Focus on key problems

Why use it?

To focus efforts on the problems that offer the greatest potential for improvement by showing their relative frequency or size in a descending bar graph.

What does it do?

- Helps a team to focus on those causes that will have the greatest impact if solved
- Based on the proven Pareto principle: 20% of the sources cause 80% of any problem
- Displays the relative importance of problems in a simple, quickly interpreted, visual format
- Helps prevent "shifting the problem" where the "solution" removes some causes but worsens others
- Progress is measured in a highly visible format that provides incentive to push on for more improvement

How do I do it?

1. **Decide which problem you want to know more about.**

   Example: Why are there delays in processing patients through the Emergency Department; what problems are people having?

2. **Choose the causes or problems that will be monitored, compared, and rank ordered by brainstorming or with existing data.**

   a) Brainstorming

   Example: What are the typical problems that cause delays in the Emergency Department?

b) Based on existing data

Example: What problems in the last month have caused delays in the Emergency Department?

3. **Choose the most meaningful unit of measurement such as frequency or cost.**

- Sometimes you don't know before the study which unit of measurement is best. Be prepared to do both frequency and cost.

Example: For the Emergency Department data the most important measure is frequency because the project team can use the information to simplify processes, improve communication or training, or solve bigger system problems.

4. **Choose the time period for the study.**

- Choose a time period that is long enough to represent the situation. Longer studies don't always translate to *better* information. Look first at volume and variety within the data.

- Make sure the scheduled time is typical in order to take into account seasonality or even different patterns within a given day or week.

Example: Review Emergency Department data for 10 weeks (May 22–August 4).

5. **Gather the necessary data on each problem category either by "real time" or reviewing historical data.**

- Whether data is gathered in "real time" or historically, Check Sheets are the easiest method for collecting data.

Example: Gather Emergency Department data based on the review of incident reports (historical).

Tip *Always* include with the source data and the final chart, the identifiers that indicate the source, location, and time period covered.

6. **Compare the relative frequency or cost of each problem category.**

   Example:

Problem Category	Frequency	Percent (%)
No wheelchair immediately available	7	2.58
Patient gets lost going to x-ray	11	4.06
Triage nurse not at triage desk	66	24.35
Phlebotomist not immediately available	42	15.50
MD must go to x-ray to review films with radiologist	21	7.75
ED room not yet cleaned, so patient can't be put in room	9	3.32
Nurses/MDs don't know which patients have been in ED for how long	35	12.92
Patient awaiting lab results that have to be sent to outside lab	11	4.06
Patient treated in ED rather than admitted	13	4.80
Patient awaiting admission to med/surg unit and bed not yet available	46	16.97
Other	10	3.69
Total	**271**	

7. **List the problem categories on the horizontal line and frequencies on the vertical line.**

   - List the categories in descending order from left to right on the horizontal line with bars above each problem category to indicate its frequency or cost. List the unit of measure on the vertical line.

8. **(Optional) Draw the cumulative percentage line showing the portion of the total that each problem category represents.**

   a) On the vertical line (opposite the raw data, #, $, etc.), record 100% opposite the total number and 50% at the halfway point. Fill in the remaining percentages drawn to scale.

b) Starting with the highest problem category, draw a dot or mark an x at the upper righthand corner of the bar.

- Add the total of the next problem category to the first and draw a dot above that bar showing both the cumulative number and percentage. Connect the dots and record the remaining cumulative totals until 100% is reached.

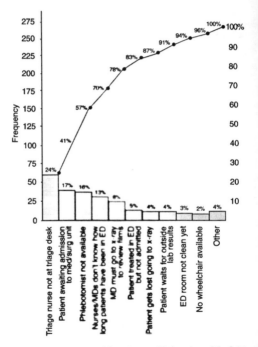

Information provided courtesy of Jim Salsbury

©1994, 2005, 2008 GOAL/QPC

9. Interpret the results.

- *Generally*, the tallest bars indicate the biggest contributors to the overall problem. Dealing with these problem categories first therefore makes common sense. *But* the most frequent or expensive is not always the most important. Always ask: What has the most impact on the goals of our business and customers?

Variations

The Pareto Chart is one of the most widely and creatively used improvement tools. The variations used most frequently are:

A. **Major Cause Breakdowns** in which the "tallest bar" is broken into subcauses in a second, linked Pareto.

B. **Before and After** in which the "new Pareto" bars are drawn side by side with the original Pareto, showing the effect of a change. It can be drawn as one chart or two separate charts.

C. **Change the Source of Data** in which data is collected on the same problem but from different departments, locations, equipment, and so on, and shown in side-by-side Pareto Charts.

D. **Change Measurement Scale** in which the same categories are used but measured differently. Typically "cost" and "frequency" are alternated.

Pareto
A. Major Cause Breakdowns

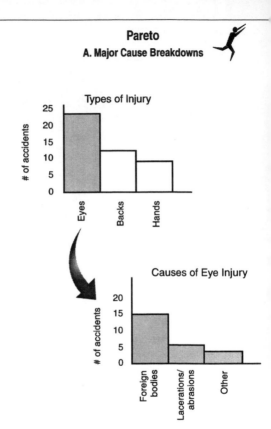

Pareto

B. Before and After

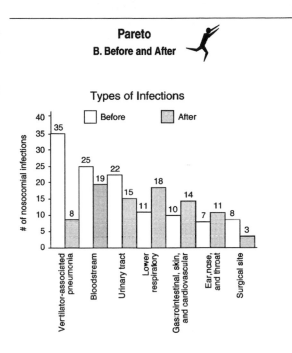

Types of Infections

Legend: □ Before   ▨ After

# of nosocomial infections (y-axis): 0 to 40

Type of Infection	Before	After
Ventilator-associated pneumonia	35	8
Bloodstream	25	19
Urinary tract	22	15
Lower respiratory	11	18
Gastrointestinal, skin, and cardiovascular	10	14
Ear, nose, and throat	7	11
Surgical site	8	3

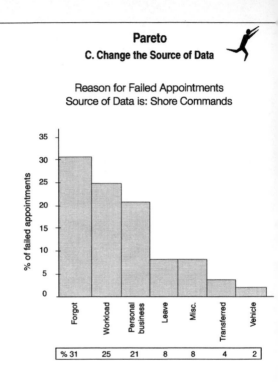

Reason for Failed Appointments
Source of Data is: Shore Commands

| % | 31 | 25 | 21 | 8 | 8 | 4 | 2 |

*Information provided courtesy of
U.S. Navy, Naval Dental Center, San Diego*

Reason for Failed Appointments
Source of Data is: Fleet Commands

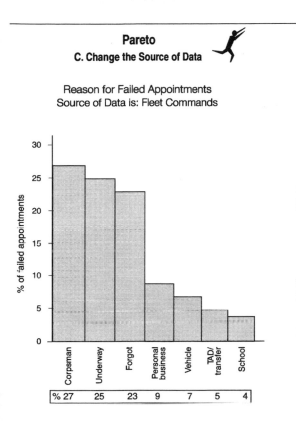

Information provided courtesy of
U.S. Navy, Naval Dental Center, San Diego

Pareto

D. Change Measurement Scale

Medical Billing Customer Complaints

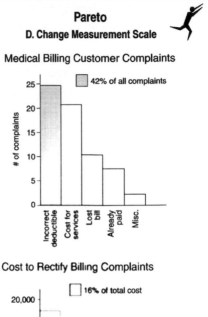

Cost to Rectify Billing Complaints

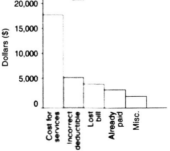

Prioritization Matrices
Weighing your options

Why use it?

To narrow down options through a systematic approach of comparing choices by selecting, weighting, and applying criteria.

What does it do?

- Quickly surfaces basic disagreements so they may be resolved up front
- Forces a team to focus on the best thing(s) to do, and not everything they could do, dramatically increasing the chances for implementation success
- Limits "hidden agendas" by surfacing the criteria as a necessary part of the process
- Increases the chance of follow-through because consensus is sought at each step in the process (from criteria to conclusions)
- Reduces the chances of selecting someone's "pet project"

How do I do it?

There are three methods for constructing Prioritization Matrices. The outline that follows indicates typical situations for using each method. Only the "Full Analytical Criteria Method" is discussed here. The others are covered fully in *The Memory Jogger Plus+*®.

Full Analytical Criteria Method

Typically used when:

- Smaller teams are involved (3–8 people)
- Options are few (5–10 choices)
- There are relatively few criteria (3–6 items)
- Complete consensus is needed
- The stakes are high if the plan fails

Consensus Criteria Method

This method follows the same steps as in the Full Analytical Criteria Method except the Consensus Criteria Method uses a combination of weighted voting, and ranking is used instead of paired comparisons.

Typically used when:

- Larger teams are involved (8 or more people)
- Options are many (10–20 choices)
- There are a significant number of criteria (6–15 items)
- Quick consensus is needed to proceed

Combination ID/Matrix Method

This method is different from the other two methods because it is based on cause and effect, rather than criteria.

Typically used when:

- Interrelationships among options are high and finding the option with the greatest impact is critical

©1994, 2005, 2008 GOAL/QPC

Full Analytical Criteria Method

1. **Agree on the ultimate goal to be achieved in a clear, concise sentence.**
   - If no other tools are used as input, produce a clear goal statement through consensus. This statement strongly affects which criteria are used.

   > Choose a new MRI scanner
   > for the hospital

2. **Create the list of criteria.**
   - Brainstorm the list of criteria or review previous documents or guidelines that are available (e.g., corporate goals, budget-related guidelines).

   > - Cost
   > - Patient comfort
   > - Image quality
   > - Speed

   Tip The team *must reach consensus* on the final criteria and their meanings or the process is likely to fail!

3. **Using an L-shaped matrix, weight each criterion against each other.**
   - Reading across from the vertical axis, compare each criterion to those on the horizontal axis.
   - Each time a weight (e.g., 1, 5, 10) is recorded in a row cell, its reciprocal value (e.g., $\frac{1}{5}$, $\frac{1}{10}$) must be recorded in the corresponding column cell.
   - Total each horizontal row and convert to a relative decimal value known as the "criteria weighting."

Criterion vs. Criterion

Criteria \ Criteria	Cost	Patient comfort	Image quality	Speed	Row Total	Relative Decimal Value
Cost		$\frac{1}{5}$	$\frac{1}{10}$	5	5.3	.15
Patient comfort	5		$\frac{1}{5}$	5	10.2	.28
Image quality	10	5		5	20	.55
Speed	$\frac{1}{5}$	$\frac{1}{5}$	$\frac{1}{5}$		.60	.02
				Grand Total	36.1	

1 = Equally important
5 = More important
10 = Much more important
$\frac{1}{5}$ = Less important
$\frac{1}{10}$ = Much less important

Row Total
Rating scores added
Grand Total
Row totals added
Relative Decimal Value
Each row total ÷ by the grand total

4. **Compare ALL options relative to each weighted criterion.**

   - *For each criterion,* create an L-shaped matrix with all of the options on both the vertical and horizontal axis and the criteria listed in the lefthand corner of the matrix. ***There will be as many options matrices as there are criteria to be applied.***

   - Use the same rating scale (1, 5, 10) as in Step 3, *BUT* customize the wording for each criterion.

   - The relative decimal value is the "option rating."

Options vs. Each Criterion (Cost Criterion)

Cost	Purcell HD	Bloch 5.2	PCL07	Mansfield 3	Row Total	Relative Decimal Value
Purcell HD		$\frac{1}{5}$	5	$\frac{1}{10}$	5.3	.12
Bloch 5.2	5		10	$\frac{1}{5}$	15.2	.33
PCL07	$\frac{1}{5}$	$\frac{1}{10}$		$\frac{1}{10}$	.40	.01
Mansfield 3	10	5	10		25	.54

1 = Equal cost
5 = Less expensive
10 = Much less expensive
$\frac{1}{5}$ = More expensive
$\frac{1}{10}$ = Much more expensive

Grand Total: 45.9

Continue Step 4 through three more Options/Criterion matrices, like this:

Patient comfort — Image quality — Speed

Crt.	Options			
Options				

Tip The whole number (1, 5, 10) must always represent a desirable rating. In some cases this may mean "less" (e.g., cost); in others this may mean "more" (e.g., tasty).

5. **Using an L-shaped summary matrix, compare each option based on all criteria combined.**

- List all criteria on the horizontal axis and all options on the vertical axis.
- In each matrix cell multiply the "criteria weighting" of each criterion (decimal value from Step 3) by the "option rating" (decimal value from Step 4). This creates an "option score."
- Add each option score across all criteria for a row total. Divide each row total by the grand total and convert to the final decimal value. Compare these decimal values to help you decide which option to pursue.

Summary Matrix
Options vs. All Criteria

Criteria / Optns.	Cost (.15)	Patient comfort (.28)	Image quality (.55)	Speed (.02)	Row Total	Relative decimal value (RT ÷ GT)
Purcell HD	.12 x .15 (.02)	.24 x .28 (.07)	.40 x .55 (.22)	.65 x .02 (.01)	.32	.32
Bloch 5.2	.33 x .15 (.05)	.37 x .28 (.10)	.10 x .55 (.06)	.22 x .02 (0)	.22	.22
PCL07	.01 x .15 (0)	.37 x .28 (.10)	.49 x .55 (.27)	.12 x .02 (0)	.37	.38
Mansfield 3	.54 x .15 (.08)	.01 x .28 (0)	.01 x .55 (.01)	.01 x .02 (0)	.09	.09
				Grand Total	1.00	

.54   x   .15
(from Step 4 matrix)   (from Step 3 matrix)

(.08)
Option score

6. **Choose the best option(s) across all criteria.**

   Tip While this is more systematic than traditional decision making, it is not a science. Use common sense and judgment when options are rated very closely, but be open to nontraditional conclusions.

Variations

See *The Memory Jogger Plus+*® for full explanations of both the Consensus Criteria Method and the Combination ID/Matrix Method. The Full Analytical Criteria Method, illustrated in this book, is recommended because it encourages full discussion and consensus on critical issues. The Full Analytical Criteria Method is a simplified adaptation of an even more rigorous model known as the Analytical Hierarchy Process. It is based on the work of Thomas Saaty, which he describes in his book *Decision Making for Leaders*. In any case, use common sense to know when a situation is important enough to warrant such thorough processes.

Prioritization

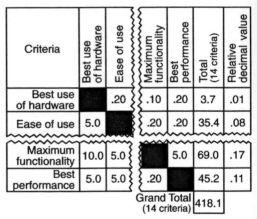

Choosing a
Medical Record-Keeping System

① Weighting criteria (described in Step 3)

This is a portion of a full matrix with 14 criteria in total.

Criteria	Best use of hardware	Ease of use	Maximum functionality	Best performance	Total (14 criteria)	Relative decimal value
Best use of hardware		.20	.10	.20	3.7	.01
Ease of use	5.0		.20	.20	35.4	.08
Maximum functionality	10.0	5.0		5.0	69.0	.17
Best performance	5.0	5.0	.20		45.2	.11
			Grand Total (14 criteria)		418.1	

Adapted from information provided courtesy of Novacor Chemicals

Note: This constructed example, illustrated on three pages, represents only a portion of the prioritization process and only a portion of the evaluation process that included 14 standard criteria.

This example continued on the next page

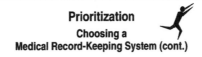
② Comparing options (described in Step 4)
These are just 2 of 14 matrices.

Best Integration –internal	System A	System B	System C	Total	Relative decimal value
System A		1.00	1.00	2.00	.33
System B	1.00		1.00	2.00	.33
System C	1.00	1.00		2.00	.33
			Grand Total	6.00	

Lowest ongoing cost	System A	System B	System C	Total	Relative decimal value
System A		.10	.20	.30	.02
System B	10.00		5.00	15.00	.73
System C	5.00	.20		5.20	.25
			Grand Total	20.50	

Adapted from information provided courtesy of Novacor Chemicals

This example continued on the next page

③ Summarize option ratings across all criteria
(described in Step 5)

This is a portion of a full matrix with 14 criteria in total.

Criteria / Options	Easy to use (.08)	Best integration int. (.09)	Lowest ongoing cost (.08)	Total (across 14 criteria)	Relative decimal value
System A	.03 (.01)	.33 (.03)	.02 (0)	.16	.18
System B	.48 (.04)	.33 (.03)	.73 (.06)	.30	.33
System C	.48 (.04)	.33 (.03)	.25 (.02)	.44	.49
			Grand Total	.90	

Adapted from information provided courtesy of Novacor Chemicals

Result: System C was chosen. Even though many team members were initially apprehensive about using this system, the prioritization process changed their minds and prevented them from biasing the final decision.

Process Capability
Measuring conformance to customer requirements

Why use it?

To determine whether a process, given its natural variation, is capable of meeting established customer requirements or specifications.

What does it do?

- Helps a team answer the question, "Is the process capable?"
- Helps to determine if there has been a change in the process
- Helps to determine percent of product or service not meeting customer requirements

How do I do it?

1. **Determine the process grand average, $\bar{\bar{X}}$, and the average range, $\bar{R}$.**

   - Use a stable Control Chart, which means the process is stable and normally distributed.

2. **Determine the Upper Specification Limit (USL) and the Lower Specification Limit (LSL).**

   - The USL and LSL are based on customer requirements. Recognize that these specification limits are based *solely* on customer requirements and do not reflect the capacity of the process.

3. **Calculate the process standard deviation.**

   - Process cability is based on individual points from a process under study. Information from a Control Chart can be used to estimate the process' average and variation (standard deviation, s).

- σ is a measure of the process (population) standard deviation and can be estimated from information on the Control Chart by

$$\hat{\sigma} = \frac{\bar{R}}{d_2} \text{ or } \hat{\sigma} = \frac{\bar{s}}{c_4}$$

where $\bar{R}$ and $\bar{s}$ are the averages of the subgroup ranges and standard deviations and d_2 and c_4 are the associated constant values based on the subgroup sample sizes. See the Table of Constants in Control Charts.

- The process average is estimated simply by $\bar{\bar{X}}, \tilde{\bar{X}}, \bar{X}$.

4. Calculate the process capability.

- To measure the degree to which a process is or is not capable of meeting customer requirements, capability indices have been developed to com-pare the distribution of your process in relation to the specification limits.

- A stable process can be represented by a measure of its variation—six standard deviations. Comparing six standard deviations of the process variation to the customer specifications provides a measure of capability. Some measures of capability include C_p and its inverse C_r, C_{pl}, C_{pu} and C_{pk}.

C_p (simple process capability)

$$C_p = \frac{USL - LSL}{6\,\hat{\sigma}}$$

Tip While C_p relates the spread of the process relative to the specification width, it *DOES NOT* look at how well the process average is centered to the target value.

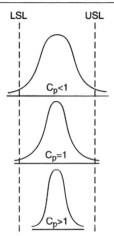

The process variation exceeds specification. Defectives are being made.

The process is just meeting specification. A minimum of .3% defectives will be made, more if the process is not centered.

The process variation is less than specification; however, defectives might be made if the process is not centered on the target value.

C_{pl}, C_{pu}, and C_{pk} (process capability indices)

The indices C_{pl} and C_{pu} (for single-sided specification limits) and C_{pk} (for two-sided specification limits) measure not only the process variation with respect to the allowable specification, they also take into account the location of the process average. C_{pk} is considered a measure of the process capability and is taken as the smaller of either C_{pl} or C_{pu}

$$C_{pl} = \frac{\bar{\bar{X}} - LSL}{3\,\hat{\sigma}} \qquad C_{pu} = \frac{USL - \bar{\bar{X}}}{3\,\hat{\sigma}} \qquad C_{pk} = \min\{C_{pl}, C_{pu}\}$$

Tip If the process is near normal and in statistical control, C_{pk} can be used to estimate the expected percent of defective material. Estimating the percentages of defective material is beyond the scope of this book and can be found in statistical books.

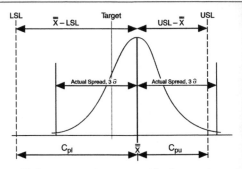

- If the process is not capable, form a team to identify and correct the common causes of the variation in the process.

  - Process capability, based on individual data of the process population, is used to determine if a process is capable of meeting customer requirements or specifications. It represents a "snapshot" of the process for some specific period of time.

  - Control Charts use small sample sizes over time and look at the averages. The control limits are natural limits of variation of the *averages within the sample*. These limits are not to be confused with specification limits, which are for *individual data points in the population*.

Variations

The construction steps described in this section are based on process capability of a Variable Data Control Chart. The process capability of an Attribute Data Control Chart is represented by the process averages $\bar{p}$, $n\bar{p}$, $\bar{c}$, and $\bar{u}$.

Process Capability

A Control Chart was maintained, producing
the following statistics:

$\bar{\bar{X}} = 212.5$ $\bar{R} = 1.2$ $n = 5$

Spec. $= 210 \pm 3$ USL $= 213$ LSL $= 207$

$$\hat{\sigma} = \frac{\bar{R}}{d_2} = \frac{1.2}{2.326} = .516$$

$$C_p = \frac{USL - LSL}{6\hat{\sigma}} = \frac{213 - 207}{6(.516)} = \frac{6}{3.096} = 1.938$$

$$C_{pl} = \frac{\bar{\bar{X}} - LSL}{3\hat{\sigma}} = \frac{212.5 - 207}{3(.516)} = \frac{5.5}{1.548} = 3.553$$

$$C_{pu} = \frac{USL - \bar{\bar{X}}}{3\hat{\sigma}} = \frac{213 - 212.5}{3(.516)} = \frac{0.5}{1.548} = 0.323$$

$$C_{pk} = \min \{C_{pl}, C_{pu}\} = 0.323$$

Because $C_{pk} < 1$, mistakes are occuring.

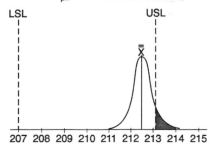

Radar Chart
Rating organization performance

Why use it?

To visually show in one graphic the size of the gaps among a number of *both current* organization performance areas *and ideal* performance areas.

What does it do?

- Makes concentrations of strengths and weaknesses visible
- Clearly displays the important categories of performance
- If done well, clearly defines full performance in each category
- Captures the different perceptions of all the team members about organization performance

How do I do it?

1. **Assemble the right team/raters.**

    Tip It is critical to get varied perspectives to avoid organization "blind spots."

2. **Select and define the rating categories.**

    - The chart can handle a wide number of categories with 5–10 categories as an average.
    - Brainstorm or bring headers from an Affinity Diagram to create the categories.
    - Define both nonperformance and full performance within each category so ratings are done consistently.

3. Construct the chart.

- Draw a large wheel on a flipchart with as many spokes as there are rating categories.
- Write down each rating category at the end of each spoke around the perimeter of the wheel.
- Mark each spoke on a zero to "n" scale with "0" at the center equal to "no performance" and the highest number on the scale at the outer ring equal to "full performance." Performance can be measured either objectively or subjectively.

4. Rate all performance categories.

a) **Individual:** Each person rates in silence, using multicolored markers or adhesive labels directly on the flipchart.

b) **Team:** Through consensus or an average of individual scores, get a team rating. Take into account both the clustering and the spread of the individual ratings.

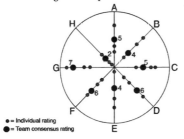

● = Individual rating
⬤ = Team consensus rating

Tip Make the team rating highly visible on the chart. Be sure to differentiate the team ratings from individual ratings on the chart by color or type of mark.

5. **Connect the team ratings for each category and highlight as needed.**

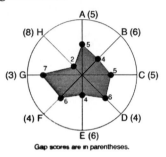

Gap scores are in parentheses.

Tip A gap score can be added to each category by subtracting the team rating score from the highest number on the rating scale (e.g., on a scale of "10," a team rating of "4" produces a gap score of "6" in categories B and E.)

6. **Interpret and use the results.**
   - The overall ratings identify gaps within each category but not the relative importance of the categories themselves. Work on the biggest gap in the most critical **category.**
   - Post the resulting Radar Chart in a prominent place, review progress regularly, and update the chart accordingly. It is a great visual "report card."

Radar

Analysis of Gaps
in the Implementation
of Strategies

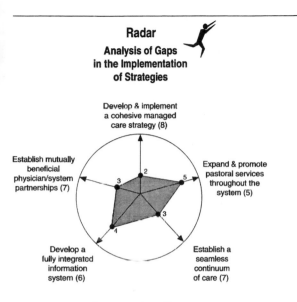

Gap scores are in parentheses.

Adapted from information provided by
Methodist Healthcare System, San Antonio, Texas,
and Our Lady of Lourdes Medical Center, Camden, New Jersey

Run Chart
Tracking trends

Why use it?

To allow a team to study observed data (a performance measure of a process) for trends or patterns over a specified period of time.

What does it do?

- Monitors the performance of one or more processes over time to detect trends, shifts, or cycles
- Allows a team to compare a performance measure before and after implementation of a solution to measure its impact
- Focuses attention on truly vital changes in the process
- Tracks useful information for predicting trends

How do I do it?

1. **Decide on the process performance measure.**

2. **Gather data.**
   - Generally, collect 20-25 data points to detect meaningful patterns.

3. **Create a graph with a vertical line (y axis) and a horizontal line (x axis).**
   - On the vertical line (y axis), draw the scale related to the variable you are measuring.
     - Arrange the y axis to cover the full range of the measurements and then some (e.g., $1\frac{1}{2}$ times the range of data).

- On the horizontal line (x axis), draw the time or sequence scale.

4. Plot the data.

- Look at the data collected. If there are no obvious trends, calculate the average or arithmetic mean. The average is the sum of the measured values divided by the number of data points. The median value can also be used but the mean is the most frequently used measure of the "centering" of the sample. (See Data Points for more information on averages.) Draw a horizontal line at the average value.

Tip Do not redraw this average line every time new data is added. Only when there has been a significant change in the process or prevailing conditions should the average be recalculated and redrawn, and then only using the data points after the verified change.

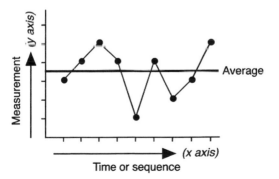

5. **Interpret the chart.**
   - Note the position of the average line. Is it where it should be relative to a customer need or specification? Is it where you want it relative to your business objective?

   Tip A danger in using a Run Chart is the tendency to see every variation in data as being important. The Run Chart should be used to focus on truly vital changes in the process. Simple tests can be used to look for meaningful trends and patterns. These tests are found in Control Charts in the "Determining if Your Process is Out of Control" section. Remember that for more sophisticated uses, a Control Chart is invaluable because it is simply a Run Chart with statistically based limits.

Run Chart
Emergency Room Admissions

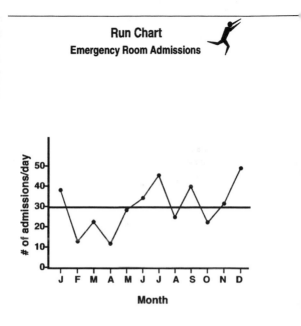

Scatter Diagram
Measuring relationships between variables

Why use it?

To study and identify the possible relationship between the changes observed in two different sets of variables.

What does it do?

- Supplies the data to confirm a hypothesis that two variables are related
- Provides both a visual and statistical means to test the strength of a potential relationship
- Provides a good follow-up to a Cause & Effect Diagram to find out if there is more than just a consensus connection between causes and the effect

How do I do it?

1. **Collect 50–100 paired samples of data that you think may be related and construct a data sheet.**

Patient	Average Session Rating (on a 1–5 scale)	Average Experience of Phlebotomist (days)
1	4.2	220
2	3.7	270
3	4.3	270
•	•	•
•	•	•
•	•	•
40	3.9	625

Theory: There is a possible relationship between the number of days of experience the phlebotomist has received and the ratings of patient sessions.

©1994, 2005, 2008 GOAL/QPC

2. Draw the horizontal (x axis) and vertical (y axis) lines of the diagram.

- The measurement scales generally increase as you move up the vertical axis and to the right on the horizontal axis.

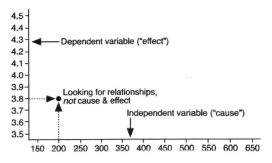

3. Plot the data on the diagram.

- If values are repeated, circle that point as many times as appropriate.

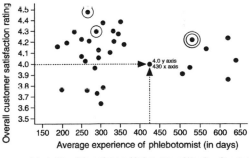

Adapted from information provided courtesy of Hamilton Standard

4. **Interpret the data.**
   - There are many levels of analysis that can be applied to Scatter Diagram data. Any basic statistical process control text, like Kaoru Ishikawa's *Guide to Quality Control*, describes additional correlation tests. It is important to note that all of the examples in this chapter are based on straight-line correlations. There are a number of non-linear patterns that can be routinely encountered (e.g., $y = e^x$, $y = x^2$). These types of analyses are beyond the scope of this book.
   - The following five illustrations show the various patterns and meanings that Scatter Diagrams can have. The example used is the patient satisfaction session assessment previously shown. The patterns have been altered for illustrative purposes. Pattern #3 is the actual sample.

   Tip The Scatter Diagram *does not predict* cause and effect relationships. It only shows the strength of the relationship between two variables. The stronger the relationship, the greater the likelihood that change in one variable will affect change in another variable.

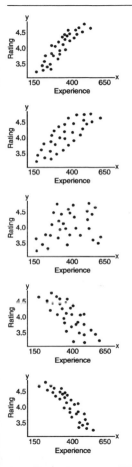

1. Positive Correlation. An increase in y may depend on an increase in x. Satisfaction ratings are likely to increase as experience increases.

2. Possible Positive Correlation. If x is increased, y may increase somewhat. Other variables may be involved in the level of rating in addition to experience.

3. No Correlation. There is no demonstrated connection between experience and satisfaction ratings.

4. Possible Negative Correlation. As x is increased, y may decrease somewhat. Other variables, besides experience, may also be affecting ratings.

5. Negative Correlation. A decrease in y may depend on an increase in x. Satisfaction ratings are likely to fall as experience increases.

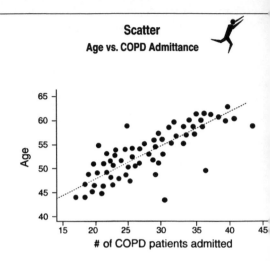

Scatter
Age vs. COPD Admittance

Adapted from information provided courtesy of AT&T and Natalie Twaddel, RN, BSN, RNC

 **Team Guidelines**
From "me" to "we"

Starting Teams

The most critical task for any new team is to establish its purpose, process, and measures of team progress. Once the team has developed the following guidelines and charters specific to its purpose, they should be recorded on a flipchart and posted at each team meeting for reference.

- **Develop a team behavior charter.**
  - *Ground rules.* Develop consensus ground rules of acceptable and unacceptable individual and team behavior.
  - *Decision making.* Determine whether decisions will be made by consensus, majority rule, or anarchy! Discuss whether there are, or should be, exceptions to when the team should not follow its usual process.
  - *Communication.* Recognize the value of listening and constructive feedback, and make the effort, every day, to communicate constructively!
  - *Roles and participation.* Discuss how the team will choose a leader, and generally how the team process will be led. The individuals and team must take responsibility to encourage equal participation.
  - *Values.* Acknowledge and accept the unique insight of each member of the team.

- **Develop a purpose charter.**
  - Establish the answer to why the team exists.

- Bring together the individuals who would work well together as a team. Determine whether each person has the knowledge, skills, and influence required to participate effectively on the team.
- The team should discuss who its customers are. If the team has multiple customers, decide which customers have the highest priority, or at least how their needs will be balanced.

- **Develop measures of team progress.**
  - Discuss and agree on the desired signals, which the team can assess both objectively and subjectively, that will indicate the team is making progress.
  - Discuss and agree on the types of measures and outcomes that will indicate the team has reached success or failure.
  - Estimate the date when the project should be completed.

Maintaining Momentum

Many teams enjoy terrific starts and then soon fizzle. The real challenge is to keep a team focused on its purpose and not the histories of its members and their relationships to one another.

- **Agree on the improvement model to use.**
  - *Standard steps*. Use your organization's standard step-by-step improvement process or choose from the many published options. (See the Improvement Storyboard in the Problem Solving/Process Improvement Model section for one such standard process.)

- *Data.* Gather relevant data to analyze the current situation. Define what you know, and what you need to know, but know when to stop. Learn, as a team, to say when your work is good enough to proceed to the next step in the process.
- *Develop a plan.* Use your organization's standard improvement model to provide the overall structure of a project plan. Estimate times for each step and for the overall project. Monitor and revise the plans as needed.

- **Use proven methods based on both data and knowledge.**
  - *Data-based methods.* Use tools in this booklet (e.g., Run Chart, Pareto Chart) that reveal patterns within data. These tools often take the emotion out of discussions and keep the process moving.
  - *Knowledge-based methods.* Many of the methods in this booklet (e.g., Affinity Diagram, Interrelationship Digraph) help to generate and analyze ideas to reveal the important information within. They help create consensus, which is the ideal energy source for a team.

- **Manage team dynamics.**
  - *Use facilitators.* A facilitator is someone who monitors and helps team members to keep their interactions positive and productive. This is the stage when a facilitator can help the team stay focused on its purpose while improving its working relationship.

- *Manage conflict.* As teams grow, so do conflicts. This is a natural process as communication becomes more open. The entire team can learn techniques for conflict resolution and use the facilitator as a resource.

- *Recognize agreement.* Managing agreement is often as much of an effort as managing disagreement. Test for agreement often and write down the points of agreement as they occur.

- *Encourage fair participation.* Each team member must eventually take responsibility for participating consistently in all discussions. Likewise, the entire team should be constantly working to "pull back" the dominant members and draw out the quieter members.

Ending Teams/Projects

Most teams and all projects must eventually end. Both often end in unsatisfactory ways or don't "officially end" at all. Before ending, the team should review the following checklist:

☐ We checked our results against our original goals and customer needs.

☐ We identified any remaining tasks to be done.

☐ We established responsibility for monitoring the change over time.

☐ We documented and trained people, when necessary, in the new process.

- [ ] We communicated the changes to everyone affected by them.

- [ ] We reviewed our own team's accomplishments for areas of improvement.

- [ ] We celebrated the efforts of the team with a lunch, newsletter article, special presentation to the company, or other expression of celebration.

- [ ] We feel proud of our contribution and accomplishments, our new capabilities, and our newly defined relationships with coworkers.

Conducting Effective Meetings

Preparation:
- Decide on the purpose of the meeting.
- Develop a meeting plan (who, what, where, when, how many).
- Identify the meeting leader.
- Prepare and distribute the agenda.
- Set up the meeting area.

Beginning:
- Start on time.
- Introduce the meeting leader.
- Allow team members to introduce themselves.
- Ask for a volunteer timekeeper.
- Ask for a volunteer recorder.
- Review, change, order the agenda.
- Establish time limits.
- Review prior meeting action items.

Meeting Etiquette:
- Raise your hand and be recognized before speaking.
- Be brief and to the point.
- Make your point calmly.
- Keep an open mind.
- Listen without bias.
- Understand what is said.
- Avoid side conversations.
- Respect other opinions.
- Avoid personal agendas.
- Come prepared to do what's good for the company.
- Have fun.

Ending:
- Develop action items (who, what, when, how).
- Summarize the meeting with the group.
- Establish the date and time for a follow-up meeting.
- Evaluate the meeting.
- End on time.
- Clean the meeting area.

Next Steps:
- Prepare and distribute the meeting activity report.
- Follow up on action items.
- Go to "Preparation."

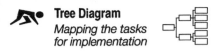

Tree Diagram
*Mapping the tasks
for implementation*

Why use it?

To break any broad goal, graphically, into increasing levels of detailed actions that must or could be done to achieve the stated goals.

What does it do?

- Encourages team members to expand their thinking when creating solutions. Simultaneously, this tool keeps everyone linked to the overall goals and subgoals of a task

- Allows all participants (and reviewers outside the team) to check all of the logical links and completeness at every level of plan detail

- Moves the planning team from theory to the real world

- Reveals the *real* level of complexity involved in the achievement of any goal, making potentially overwhelming projects manageable, as well as uncovering unknown complexity

How do I do it?

1. **Choose the Tree Diagram goal statement.**

> **Goal: Establish an experiential education program**

- Typical sources:
  - The root cause/driver identified in an Interrelationship Digraph (ID)
  - An Affinity Diagram with the headers as major subgoals
  - Any assignment given to an individual or team
- When used in conjunction with other management and planning tools, the most typical source is the root cause/driver identified in the ID.

Tip Regardless of the source, work hard to create—through consensus—a clear, action-oriented statement.

2. Assemble the right team.

- The team should consist of action planners with detailed knowledge of the goal topic. The team should take the Tree only to the level of detail that the team's knowledge will allow. Be prepared to hand further details to others.
- Four-to-six people is the ideal group size but the Tree Diagram is appropriate for larger groups as long as the ideas are visible and the session is well facilitated.

3. Generate the major Tree headings, which are the major subgoals to pursue.

- The simplest method for creating the highest, or first, level of detail is to brainstorm the major task areas. These are the major "means" by which the goal statement will be achieved.

- To encourage creativity, it is often helpful to do an "Action Affinity" on the goal statement. Brainstorm action statements and sort into groupings, but spend less time than usual refining the header cards. Use the header cards as the Tree's first-level subgoals.

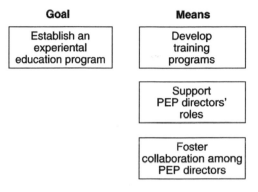

Goal	Means
Establish an experiental education program	Develop training programs
	Support PEP directors' roles
	Foster collaboration among PEP directors

Tip Use sticky notes to create the levels of detail. Draw lines only when the Tree is finished. This allows it to stay flexible until the process is finished. The Tree can be oriented from left to right, right to left, or top down.

Tip Keep the first level of detail broad, and avoid jumping to the lowest level of task. Remember: "If you start with what you already know, you'll end up where you've already been."

4. Break each major heading into greater detail.

- Working from the goal statement and first-level detail, placed either to the extreme left, right, or top of the work surface, ask of each first-level item:

  "What needs to be addressed to achieve the goal statement?"

  Repeat this question for each successive level of detail.

- Stop the breakdown of each level when there are assignable tasks or the team reaches the limit to its own expertise. Most Trees are broken out to the third level of detail (not counting the overall goal statement as a level). However, some subgoals are just simpler than others and don't require as much breakdown.

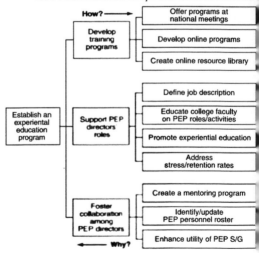

Adapted from information provided courtesy of
The American Association of Colleges of Pharmacy

5. **Review the completed Tree Diagram for logical flow and completeness.**
   - At each level of detail, ask "Is there something obvious that we have forgotten?"
   - As the Tree breaks down into greater detail (from general to specific), ask, "If I want to accomplish these results, do I really need to do these tasks?"
   - As the Tree builds into broader goals (from the specific to the general), ask, "Will these actions actually lead to these results?"
   - Draw the lines connecting the tasks.

   Tip The Tree Diagram is a great communication tool. It can be used to get input from those outside the team. The team's final task is to consider proposed changes, additions, or deletions, and to modify the Tree as appropriate.

Variations

The Process Decision Program Chart (PDPC) is a valuable tool for improving implementation through contingency planning. The PDPC, based on the Tree Diagram, involves a few simple steps.

1. **Assemble a team closest to the implementation.**

2. **Determine proposed implementation steps.**
   - List 4–10 broad steps and place them in sequence in the first Tree level.

3. **Branch likely problems off each step.**
   - Ask "What could go wrong?"

4. **Branch possible and reasonable responses off each likely problem.**

5. **Choose the most effective countermeasures and build them into a revised plan.**

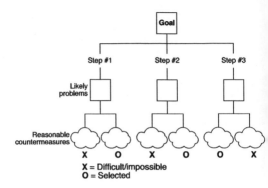

X = Difficult/impossible
O = Selected

Tree

**Factors to Determine
the Level of Care for Heart Failure Patients**

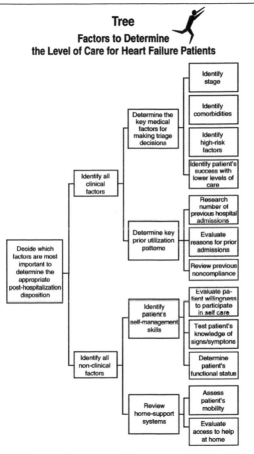

		Identify stage
	Determine the key medical factors for making triage decisions	Identify comorbidities
		Identify high-risk factors
		Identify patient's success with lower levels of care
Identify all clinical factors		Research number of previous hospital admissions
	Determine key prior utilization patterns	Evaluate reasons for prior admissions
		Review previous noncompliance

Decide which factors are most important to determine the appropriate post-hospitalization disposition

Identify all non-clinical factors

		Evaluate patient willingness to participate in self care
Identify patient's self-management skills	Test patient's knowledge of signs/symptoms
	Determine patient's functional status
Review home-support systems	Assess patient's mobility
	Evaluate access to help at home

Information provided courtesy of Partners HealthCare System, Inc.

Tree

Operating Room
Cleaning Procedure

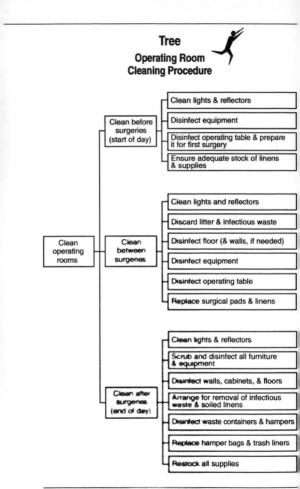

```
Clean          Clean before       ┌─ Clean lights & reflectors
operating      surgeries          ├─ Disinfect equipment
rooms          (start of day)     ├─ Disinfect operating table & prepare
                                  │   it for first surgery
                                  └─ Ensure adequate stock of linens
                                      & supplies

               Clean              ┌─ Clean lights and reflectors
               between            ├─ Discard litter & infectious waste
               surgeries          ├─ Disinfect floor (& walls, if needed)
                                  ├─ Disinfect equipment
                                  ├─ Disinfect operating table
                                  └─ Replace surgical pads & linens

               Clean after        ┌─ Clean lights & reflectors
               surgeries          ├─ Scrub and disinfect all furniture
               (end of day)       │   & equipment
                                  ├─ Disinfect walls, cabinets, & floors
                                  ├─ Arrange for removal of infectious
                                  │   waste & soiled linens
                                  ├─ Disinfect waste containers & hampers
                                  ├─ Replace hamper bags & trash liners
                                  └─ Restock all supplies
```

PDPC (Tree Variation)

Develop Product Tests Set in Both the Laboratory and Everyday Situations

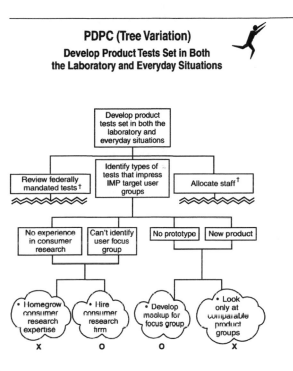

Further information exists but is not shown.

Problem-Solving/ Process-Improvement Model

Improvement Storyboard

There are many standard models for making improvements. They all attempt to provide a repeatable set of steps that a team or individual can learn and follow. The Improvement Storyboard is only *one* of many models that include typical steps using typical tools. Follow this model or any other model that creates a common language for continuous improvement within your organization.

Plan

1. Select the problem/process that will be addressed first (or next) and describe the improvement opportunity.

2. Describe the current process surrounding the improvement opportunity.

3. Describe all of the possible causes of the problem and agree on the root cause(s).

4. Develop an effective and workable solution and action plan, including targets for improvement.

Do

5. Implement the solution or process change.

Check

6. Review and evaluate the result of the change.

Act

7. Reflect and act on learnings.

Depending on your formal process structure, Step 1 may be done by a steering committee, management team, or improvement team. If you are an improvement team leader or member, be prepared to start with Step 1 *or* Step 2.

1. **Select the problem/process that will be addressed first (or next) and describe the improvement opportunity.**
   - Look for changes in quality or outcomes indicators.
   - Assemble and support the right team.
   - Review patient data.
   - Narrow down the project focus. Develop the project purpose statement.

Typical tools
Brainstorming, Affinity Diagram, Check Sheet, Control Chart, Histogram, Interrelationship Digraph, Pareto Chart, Prioritization Matrices, Process Capability, Radar Chart, Run Chart

Situation
Over the last few months, Jordan Hospital, a 600-bed tertiary care facility, has seen a two-fold increase in patient volume to the post-surgical nursing floors and Intensive Care Unit (ICU). A key measure of success for the hospital, and one on which they have proudly outperformed their competitors, has been the reduction of nosocomial infections. (Nosocomial infections are those that a patient acquires after he or she is admitted to the hospital.) However, over the last several months, infection rates have been climbing at an alarming pace. A team consisting of the infection control manager, a surgeon, the ICU nurse manager, a phlebotomist, and the HR manager convened to study the problem. They used a Run Chart to track the increase in infection rates, and created a Pareto Chart to identify the types of infections that were the most responsible for the increases.

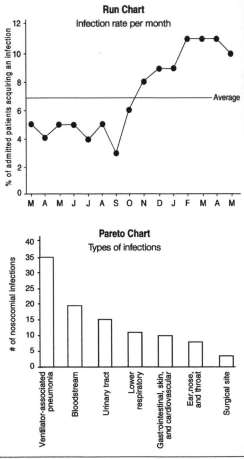

Run Chart

Infection rate per month

Pareto Chart

Types of infections

Decision

The highest percentage of infections involved ventilator-associated pneumonia (VAP). Failure in this area produced a cascade of bad quality measurements, including length of stay (LOS), morbidity rates, and procedural costs.

Project purpose statement

Reduce ventilator-associated infection rates.

2. **Describe the current process surrounding the improvement opportunity.**
   - Select the relevant process or process segment to define the scope of the project.
   - Describe the process under study.

Typical tools

Brainstorming, Macro, Top-down, and Deployment Flowcharts, Tree Diagram

Situation

The team began by reviewing the overall care process for patients on ventilators. They used a Macro Flowchart to illustrate the main steps currently in practice. Even at this high level of detail, the team had some difficulty agreeing on what the current practice was.

Macro Flowchart
Care process for patients on ventilators

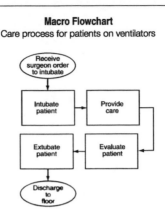

Decision
In particular, the team found inconsistencies in the timing and execution of the patient evaluation process. The evaluation process helps caregivers decide when to wean a patient from the ventilator. The longer the patient is mechanically ventilated, the higher the risk for infection.

3. **Describe all of the possible causes of the problem and agree on the root cause(s).**

   - Identify and gather helpful facts and opinions on the cause(s) of the problem.

   - Confirm opinions on root cause(s) with data whenever possible

Typical tools
Affinity Diagram, Brainstorming, C & E/Fishbone Diagram, Check Sheet, Force Field Analysis, Interrelationship Digraph, Multivoting, Nominal Group Technique, Pareto Chart, Run Chart, Scatter Diagram

Situation
The team brainstormed all of the possible causes for inconsistencies in the process and then continued to ask "Why?" so that possible root causes could emerge. The team documented their thinking with a C&E/Fishbone Diagram.

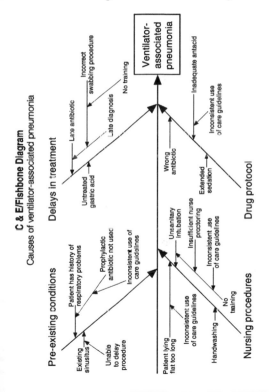

C & E/Fishbone Diagram
Causes of ventilator-associated pneumonia

Decision
The team identified two root causes:

- An inconsistent use of care guidelines for ventilated patients.
- A lack of training for new nurses and other staff in the use of those care guidelines.

Additional data showed that, because of a shortage of employees and an increase in caseload, less time was put into training the staff. As a result, many caregivers were left to come up with their own way of doing things.

4. **Develop an effective and workable solution and action plan, including targets for improvement.**
   - Define and rank solutions.
   - Plan the change process: What? Who? When?
   - Do contingency planning when dealing with new and risky plans.
   - Set targets for improvement and establish monitoring methods.

Typical tools
Activity Network Diagram, Brainstorming, Flowchart, Gantt Chart, Multivoting, Nominal Group Technique, PDPC, Prioritization Matrices, Matrix Diagram, Tree Diagram

Situation
The team used Prioritization Matrices and a Matrix Diagram to evaluate possible solutions and create a workable plan to fix the problem.

Decision

Every caregiver associated with ventilated patients was invited to offer ideas on how to better define and enforce an improved process for caring for these types of patients. The team started with Prioritization Matrices to help them select the best ideas to implement.

Prioritization Matrix

Summary matrix of options vs. all criteria

Criteria / Options	Likely to reduce infections (.35)	Acceptable to care staff (.59)	Quick to implement (.06)	Row total	Relative decimal value
Hire full-time inspector	.02 x .35 (.01)	.03 x .59 (.02)	.54 x .06 (.03)	.06	.06
Train all in care guidelines	.60 x .35 (.21)	.42 x .59 (.25)	.01 x .06 (0)	.46	.45
Link infection rates to pay	.19 x .35 (.07)	.03 x .59 (.02)	.33 x .06 (.02)	.11	.11
Redesign process for stocking bedside supplies	.19 x .35 (.07)	.52 x .59 (.31)	.11 x .06 (.01)	.39	.38
			Grand Total	1.02	

Note: **Weighting values** of each criterion come from a criteria matrix not shown.

Task options come from brainstorming sessions with caregivers.

From the Prioritization Matrices, the team selected "Train all in care guidelines" as a solution to implement immediately. They created a Gantt Chart to illustrate a timeline for the rollout of training.

Gantt Chart

Ventilator care guideline training

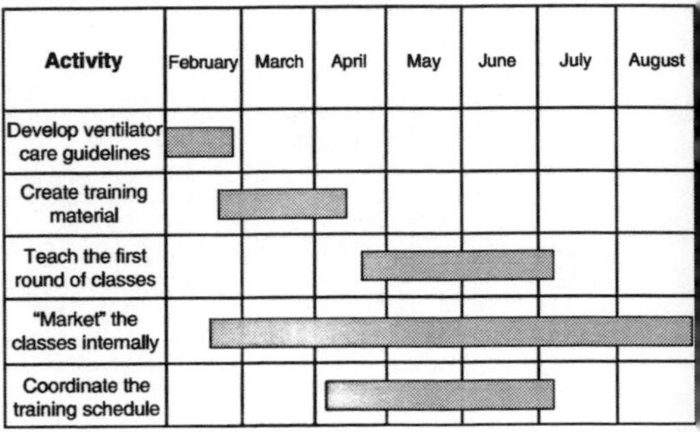
Activity
February
March
April
May
June
July
August
Develop ventilator care guidelines
Create training material
Teach the first round of classes
"Market" the classes internally
Coordinate the training schedule

Given the rapid growth in staff and the relocation of caregivers to cover staff shortages, it was sometimes unclear who was responsible for specific tasks. The team believed this confusion could interfere with the success of implementing the training, so they created a Matrix Diagram to highlight critical roles.

Matrix Diagram
Critical roles

Resource / Activity	Clark, Admin	Foley, NP	Wells, MD	Hering, HR	Cho, MD
Develop ventilator care guidelines	△	◉	△		○
Create training material	○	○		◉	
Teach the first round of classes	△	◉	◉	○	
"Market" the classes internally		○		◉	
Coordinate the training schedule	◉				

◉ = Primary responsibility

○ = Secondary responsibility

△ - Kept informed

Do

5. Implement the solution or process change.

- It is often recommended to try the solution on a small scale first.
- Follow the plan and monitor the milestones and measures.

Typical tools

Activity Network Diagram, Flowchart, Gantt Chart, Matrix Diagram, and other project management methods, as well as gathering ongoing data with Run Charts, Check Sheets, Histograms, Process Capability, and Control Charts

Situation

The team used the Responsibility Matrix and Gantt Chart they created to guide the training rollout. There were some initial problems coordinating training with busy employee schedules and finding appropriate places to practice the training.

Decision

The solution was to set up overlapping shifts for better coverage for staff, and set up a "training station" on one of the floors. Once these adjustments were made, training proceeded according to plan.

6. Review and evaluate the result of the change.

- Confirm or establish the means of monitoring the solution. Are the measures valid?
- Is the solution having the intended effect? Any unintended consequences?

Typical tools
Check Sheet, Control Chart, Flowchart, Pareto Chart, Run Chart

Situation
The team continued to track overall infection rates for six months on a Run Chart, and used a Pareto Chart to compare the rates for VAP before and after implementation of the training plan.

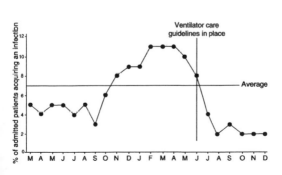

Run Chart
Infection rate per month

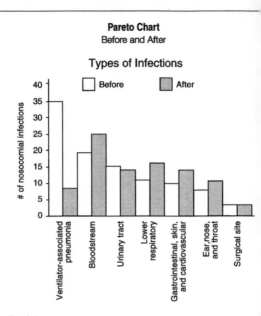

Pareto Chart
Before and After

Types of Infections

Decision

The number of ventilator-associated pneumonia cases dropped dramatically once the training was complete. During an equivalent time period, the number of these types of infections fell from 35 to 8.

7. Reflect and act on learnings.

- Assess the results and problem-solving process, and recommend changes.

- Continue the improvement process where needed; standardize where possible.

- Celebrate success.

Typical tools
Affinity Diagram, Brainstorming, Improvement Storyboard, Radar Chart

Situation
The team met six months later to evaluate their results and process. They used a Radar Chart in their assessment of the team.

Decision
The Radar Chart showed strong agreement among team members in the categories of "Results," "Use of tools," and "Impact on patients." The performance and consensus among team members were lower in both "Standardization" and "Teamwork." The team presented its storyboard to management, which resulted in an overhaul of training processes throughout the organization. The team had a party to recognize everyone who had contributed to their success, and then set about planning processes to reduce other sources of infection in the hospital.

Radar Chart
Team evaluation of itself

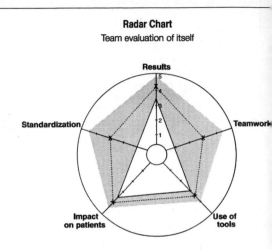

Note: The "x" mark indicates the team's average performance rating while the shaded area indicates the range of ratings within the team.